CYBER INCIDENT RESPONSE

COUNTERINTELLIGENCE AND FORENSICS FOR SECURITY INVESTIGATORS

4 BOOKS IN 1

BOOK 1
CYBER INCIDENT RESPONSE FUNDAMENTALS: A BEGINNER'S GUIDE TO COUNTERINTELLIGENCE AND FORENSICS

BOOK 2
INTERMEDIATE CYBER FORENSICS: TECHNIQUES AND TOOLS FOR SECURITY INVESTIGATORS

BOOK 3
ADVANCED COUNTERINTELLIGENCE STRATEGIES: EXPERT METHODS IN CYBER INCIDENT RESPONSE

BOOK 4
MASTERING CYBER INCIDENT RESPONSE: COMPREHENSIVE TECHNIQUES FOR ELITE SECURITY INVESTIGATORS

ROB BOTWRIGHT

Published by Rob Botwright
Library of Congress Cataloging-in-Publication Data
ISBN 978-1-83938-803-3
Cover design by Rizzo

Disclaimer

The contents of this book are based on extensive research and the best available historical sources. However, the author and publisher make no claims, promises, or guarantees about the accuracy, completeness, or adequacy of the information contained herein. The information in this book is provided on an "as is" basis, and the author and publisher disclaim any and all liability for any errors, omissions, or inaccuracies in the information or for any actions taken in reliance on such information. The opinions and views expressed in this book are those of the author and do not necessarily reflect the official policy or position of any organization or individual mentioned in this book. Any reference to specific people, places, or events is intended only to provide historical context and is not intended to defame or malign any group, individual, or entity. The information in this book is intended for educational and entertainment purposes only. It is not intended to be a substitute for professional advice or judgment. Readers are encouraged to conduct their own research and to seek professional advice where appropriate. Every effort has been made to obtain necessary permissions and acknowledgments for all images and other copyrighted material used in this book. Any errors or omissions in this regard are unintentional, and the author and publisher will correct them in future editions.

BOOK 1 - CYBER INCIDENT RESPONSE FUNDAMENTALS: A BEGINNER'S GUIDE TO COUNTERINTELLIGENCE AND FORENSICS

BOOK 2 - INTERMEDIATE CYBER FORENSICS: TECHNIQUES AND TOOLS FOR SECURITY INVESTIGATORS

BOOK 3 - ADVANCED COUNTERINTELLIGENCE STRATEGIES: EXPERT METHODS IN CYBER INCIDENT RESPONSE

BOOK 4 - MASTERING CYBER INCIDENT RESPONSE: COMPREHENSIVE TECHNIQUES FOR ELITE SECURITY INVESTIGATORS

Introduction

Welcome to the definitive guide on cyber incident response, counterintelligence, and forensics tailored specifically for security investigators. This book bundle, titled "Cyber Incident Response: Counterintelligence and Forensics for Security Investigators," comprises four comprehensive volumes meticulously curated to equip both aspiring and seasoned professionals with the knowledge, skills, and strategies essential for navigating the complex landscape of cybersecurity threats and forensic investigations.

Book 1, "Cyber Incident Response Fundamentals: A Beginner's Guide to Counterintelligence and Forensics," serves as the foundational cornerstone of this bundle. Designed for beginners, it introduces fundamental concepts, principles, and methodologies crucial for understanding cyber threats, incident detection, and initial response protocols. Readers will gain insights into the importance of proactive defense measures, incident handling procedures, and the role of forensic analysis in mitigating cyber risks.

Building upon this foundation, Book 2, "Intermediate Cyber Forensics: Techniques and Tools for Security Investigators," delves deeper into advanced forensic techniques and tools essential for conducting thorough investigations. From digital evidence acquisition and preservation to forensic analysis using specialized tools and methodologies, this volume equips investigators with practical skills to identify, analyze, and attribute cyber incidents effectively.

Book 3, "Advanced Counterintelligence Strategies: Expert Methods in Cyber Incident Response," shifts the focus to expert-level strategies employed by seasoned security professionals. It explores proactive threat hunting techniques, advanced incident response tactics, and counterintelligence strategies aimed at anticipating and thwarting sophisticated cyber threats. Readers will learn to leverage threat intelligence, develop robust defense strategies, and orchestrate coordinated responses to mitigate risks and protect organizational assets.

Finally, Book 4, "Mastering Cyber Incident Response: Comprehensive Techniques for Elite Security Investigators," consolidates the knowledge and expertise acquired throughout the series. This volume is tailored for elite security investigators seeking to refine their skills in orchestrating complex incident response operations. It covers advanced topics such as incident command systems, crisis management frameworks, and the integration of advanced technologies for enhancing incident response capabilities and organizational resilience.

Each book in this bundle is crafted to provide a progressive learning experience, from foundational principles to expert-level strategies, ensuring that readers at every stage of their cybersecurity journey find valuable insights and practical guidance. Whether you are entering the field of cybersecurity or looking to advance your career as a security investigator, this bundle equips you with the tools, methodologies, and best practices necessary to effectively detect, respond to, and mitigate the impact of cyber incidents. Through a blend of theoretical knowledge, practical insights, case studies, and hands-on exercises, "Cyber Incident Response: Counterintelligence and Forensics for Security Investigators" aims to empower readers with the skills and confidence to tackle the evolving challenges of cybersecurity with precision and effectiveness. Prepare to embark on a transformative journey that will not only deepen your understanding of cyber incident response but also elevate your capabilities as a trusted defender of digital assets and organizational integrity.

BOOK 1
CYBER INCIDENT RESPONSE FUNDAMENTALS
A BEGINNER'S GUIDE TO COUNTERINTELLIGENCE AND
FORENSICS

ROB BOTWRIGHT

Chapter 1: Introduction to Cyber Incident Response

The importance of incident response plans cannot be overstated in today's cybersecurity landscape. A well-defined and meticulously executed incident response plan is not merely a reactive measure but a proactive strategy essential for mitigating the impact of cyber incidents on organizations. At the core of any incident response plan lies the ability to swiftly detect, contain, and remediate security breaches, thereby minimizing potential damage to data, systems, and reputation. Central to the effectiveness of these plans is the clarity of roles and responsibilities assigned to incident response team members, ensuring a coordinated and efficient response in times of crisis.

Incident response plans typically begin with comprehensive risk assessments and threat modeling exercises, which help organizations identify potential vulnerabilities and prioritize critical assets. These assessments inform the development of incident response strategies tailored to specific threat scenarios, ranging from ransomware attacks to data breaches and insider threats. In practice, this means establishing incident response playbooks that outline step-by-step procedures for different types of incidents, ensuring consistency and reliability in the face of adversity.

An essential component of incident response planning is the establishment of clear communication channels both within the organization and with external stakeholders, such as law enforcement agencies, regulatory bodies, and customers. Effective communication protocols enable rapid decision-making and information sharing during an incident, facilitating a unified response effort aimed at containment and resolution. Moreover, incident response plans often include provisions for public relations and crisis management strategies to safeguard the organization's reputation and maintain stakeholder trust in the aftermath of an incident.

Technical readiness is another critical aspect of incident response planning, involving the deployment of monitoring tools, intrusion detection systems (IDS), and security information and event management (SIEM) solutions. These technologies play a pivotal role in early threat detection by monitoring network traffic, identifying anomalous behavior, and alerting incident responders to potential security breaches. Upon detection, incident responders leverage forensic analysis techniques to investigate the scope and impact of the incident, utilizing tools such as memory forensics for volatile data analysis and disk imaging for non-volatile data preservation.

In cases where malicious activities involve sophisticated malware or advanced persistent threats (APT), incident response teams may resort to malware reverse engineering to uncover the malware's functionalities and propagation methods. This process involves dissecting the code, analyzing its behavior in a controlled environment, and identifying indicators of compromise (IOCs) to strengthen defenses and prevent future incidents. Similarly, the forensic analysis of encrypted data requires specialized techniques and tools to recover and interpret information concealed by encryption algorithms, ensuring comprehensive incident response and mitigation strategies.

Incident response plans also extend their purview to encompass industrial control systems (ICS) and critical infrastructure, where the repercussions of security breaches can have far-reaching consequences on public safety and operational continuity. Mitigating risks in these environments involves adapting incident response frameworks to address specific ICS vulnerabilities and implementing protective measures, such as network segmentation and access controls, to safeguard operational technologies (OT) from cyber threats.

Continuous improvement is fundamental to the efficacy of incident response plans, necessitating regular testing, evaluation, and refinement through incident response exercises and tabletop simulations. These simulations simulate realistic scenarios to assess the readiness of incident response teams, identify gaps in procedures, and refine communication protocols. Lessons learned from these exercises are then incorporated into updated incident response playbooks, ensuring that organizations remain agile and adaptive in the face of evolving cyber threats.

In summary, incident response plans represent a cornerstone of cybersecurity resilience, providing organizations with the foresight and capability to effectively mitigate and manage security incidents. By combining strategic planning, technical readiness, and proactive measures, incident response plans empower organizations to minimize the impact of cyber incidents, safeguard sensitive data, and preserve stakeholder trust. As cyber threats continue to evolve in complexity and sophistication, the importance of robust incident response planning cannot be understated, serving as a proactive defense mechanism against the ever-present dangers of the digital landscape. Key elements of an incident response team encompass a multifaceted approach to handling cybersecurity incidents effectively and efficiently. At its core, an incident response team is comprised of individuals with specialized skills and responsibilities tailored to different phases of incident management, from detection and analysis to containment, eradication, and recovery. One of the fundamental components of an incident response team is the designation of clear roles and responsibilities, ensuring each team member understands their tasks and contributions during an incident. For instance, a typical incident response team structure includes roles such as Incident Coordinator, who oversees the overall response efforts and ensures coordination among team members, and Forensic Analysts, responsible for conducting in-depth analysis of digital evidence to determine the scope and impact of the incident. These roles are crucial in maintaining organization and efficiency during high-stress situations, ensuring a cohesive response that minimizes downtime and mitigates potential damage.

Technical expertise is another essential element within an incident response team, with members possessing skills in areas such as network security, digital forensics, malware analysis, and threat intelligence. For example, Network Security Analysts play a pivotal role in monitoring network traffic using tools like Wireshark or tcpdump to identify suspicious activities or anomalies that may indicate a security breach. Upon detection, these analysts may deploy command-line tools like `tcpdump -i eth0` to capture and analyze network packets in real-time, helping to pinpoint the source and nature of the intrusion. Similarly, Digital Forensic Analysts employ tools such as `Autopsy` or `Sleuth Kit` for disk imaging and data recovery, enabling them to reconstruct digital artifacts and uncover evidence crucial to understanding the incident's timeline and impact.

Effective communication is another critical element of an incident response team, facilitating timely information sharing and decision-making throughout the incident lifecycle. Communication channels must be established both within the team and with external stakeholders, such as senior management, legal counsel, IT support staff, and law enforcement agencies. This ensures that all parties are informed of incident developments, escalation procedures, and mitigation strategies. Tools like Slack or Microsoft Teams are often utilized for real-time communication among team members, allowing for rapid dissemination of updates and collaborative problem-solving during incidents. Furthermore, incident response team members must be adept at crafting clear and concise incident reports, detailing the incident's timeline, findings, and remediation actions taken. This documentation not only serves as a record of the incident response process but also informs post-incident reviews and lessons learned sessions aimed at improving future response efforts.

Collaboration and teamwork are integral to the success of an incident response team, fostering a culture of trust, respect, and shared responsibility among its members. Cross-functional collaboration allows team members to leverage diverse perspectives and expertise in developing comprehensive incident response strategies tailored to specific threats and vulnerabilities. For example, during incident debriefings or "post-mortems," teams may utilize techniques like root cause analysis (RCA) to identify underlying causes of incidents and recommend preventive measures or process improvements. Command-line tools such as `grep` or `awk` may be used to parse log files and pinpoint the exact sequence of events leading to the incident, aiding in RCA efforts and informing proactive security measures.

Continuous training and skill development are essential elements of an incident response team, ensuring that members remain proficient in emerging threats, technologies, and incident response techniques. Training programs may include scenario-based simulations, tabletop exercises, and hands-on workshops designed to simulate real-world incidents and test response capabilities. These exercises allow team members to practice their roles and responsibilities in a controlled environment, identify areas for improvement, and refine incident response procedures. Moreover, certification programs such as Certified Incident Handler (GCIH) or Certified Computer Examiner (CCE) provide formal recognition of expertise in incident response and digital forensics, enhancing the credibility and proficiency of team members within the cybersecurity community.

Lastly, proactive measures such as threat intelligence sharing and vulnerability management are crucial elements of an incident response team's strategy, enabling organizations to preemptively identify and mitigate potential threats before they escalate into full-blown incidents. Threat intelligence platforms like `MISP` or `ThreatConnect` aggregate and analyze threat data from various sources, providing actionable insights into emerging threats, adversary tactics, and indicators of compromise (IOCs). Incident response teams leverage this intelligence to strengthen defensive strategies, update detection mechanisms, and proactively hunt for signs of compromise within their environments. Additionally, vulnerability management tools such as `OpenVAS` or `Nessus` scan network infrastructure and applications for known vulnerabilities, allowing teams to prioritize patching and remediation efforts based on risk severity and potential impact.

In summary, the key elements of an incident response team encompass a blend of organizational structure, technical expertise, effective communication, collaboration, continuous training, and proactive measures. By integrating these elements into a cohesive and well-coordinated framework, organizations can enhance their resilience against cyber threats, mitigate the impact of security incidents, and maintain operational continuity in an increasingly complex and dynamic threat landscape.

Chapter 2: Understanding Cyber Threats and Attacks

Types of cyber threat actors encompass a diverse array of individuals, groups, and entities with varying motivations, capabilities, and methods, each posing distinct challenges to cybersecurity professionals and organizations worldwide. One prominent category of cyber threat actors includes **Hacktivists**, who are driven by ideological or political motives and often target organizations or individuals perceived as adversaries. Hacktivist groups such as Anonymous have been known to conduct distributed denial-of-service (DDoS) attacks against government agencies, corporations, and institutions to protest or raise awareness about social and political issues. These attacks can disrupt services, damage reputation, and impose significant operational costs on targeted entities, highlighting the disruptive nature of hacktivism in the digital age.

Another category of cyber threat actors comprises **Cybercriminals**, who operate with the primary goal of financial gain through illicit activities such as **Phishing** campaigns, **Ransomware** attacks, and **Identity Theft**. Phishing involves the use of deceptive emails or websites to trick individuals into divulging sensitive information, such as login credentials or financial details, which cybercriminals then exploit for fraudulent purposes. Techniques like **Social Engineering**, where attackers manipulate psychological factors to coerce individuals into revealing information or performing actions that compromise security, are often employed in phishing attacks. Mitigating these threats requires organizations to implement robust email filtering solutions and conduct regular security awareness training to educate employees about recognizing and avoiding phishing attempts.

Ransomware attacks, another favored tactic of cybercriminals, involve encrypting victims' data and demanding ransom payments in exchange for decryption keys. To mitigate the risk of ransomware attacks, organizations should regularly backup critical data and systems, implement network segmentation to limit the spread of infections, and deploy endpoint protection solutions that detect and block ransomware before it can execute. In cases where ransomware successfully encrypts data, incident response teams may leverage tools like **WannaCryDecryptor** to decrypt files without paying ransom, provided the ransomware variant is decryptable.

Organized **Cybercrime Syndicates** represent another sophisticated type of cyber threat actor, leveraging a hierarchical structure, specialized skills, and extensive resources to orchestrate complex cyberattacks for profit. These syndicates often operate on a global scale, utilizing underground forums and black markets to buy, sell, and trade stolen data, exploit kits, and hacking tools. For instance, the **Dark Web** marketplace allows cybercriminals to purchase malware-as-a-service (MaaS) subscriptions or rent botnets for launching DDoS attacks, demonstrating the commercialization of cybercrime and its impact on cybersecurity landscape.

State-sponsored cyber threat actors, also known as **Advanced Persistent Threats (APTs)**, represent another formidable category with the backing and resources of nation-states to conduct espionage, sabotage, or geopolitical agendas. APT groups like **APT28** (Fancy Bear) and **APT29** (Cozy Bear) have been linked to cyber espionage campaigns targeting governments, military organizations, and critical infrastructure sectors worldwide. These actors employ sophisticated techniques such as **Zero-Day Exploits** and **Custom Malware** to infiltrate target networks, exfiltrate sensitive information, and maintain persistence over extended periods. Mitigating APT threats requires organizations to implement defense-in-depth strategies, including network segmentation, endpoint detection and response (EDR) solutions, and continuous monitoring for anomalous activities indicative of APT operations.

Insider threats constitute another significant category of cyber threat actors, encompassing individuals with legitimate access to an organization's systems, data, and infrastructure who intentionally or unintentionally compromise security. Insider threats can manifest as **Malicious Insiders**, who abuse their privileges to steal intellectual property, sabotage systems, or perpetrate fraud, and **Negligent Insiders**, whose inadvertent actions, such as clicking on phishing links or mishandling sensitive data, inadvertently expose organizations to security risks. To mitigate insider threats, organizations should implement robust access controls, monitor employee activities for suspicious behavior, and enforce security policies and procedures that emphasize data protection and confidentiality.

Lastly, **Nation-State Actors** represent the most sophisticated and well-resourced cyber threat actors, operating with the backing and support of governments to conduct cyber espionage, cyber warfare, and geopolitical influence operations. These actors possess advanced capabilities in offensive cyber operations, including the development of **Advanced Cyber Weapons** like Stuxnet, a sophisticated malware designed to sabotage Iran's nuclear program. Nation-state actors often target critical infrastructure, government agencies, defense contractors, and multinational corporations to steal sensitive information, disrupt operations, or gain strategic advantages in global conflicts.

In response to the evolving threat landscape posed by these diverse cyber threat actors, organizations and cybersecurity professionals must adopt a proactive approach to cybersecurity, emphasizing threat intelligence gathering, vulnerability management, and incident response preparedness. By understanding the motivations, tactics, and techniques employed by different types of cyber threat actors, organizations can better defend against and mitigate the impact of cyberattacks, safeguarding sensitive data, maintaining operational resilience, and preserving stakeholder trust in an increasingly interconnected digital world. Common methods of cyber attack encompass a wide range of techniques and strategies employed by malicious actors to compromise systems, steal sensitive data, and disrupt operations, highlighting the persistent and evolving nature of cybersecurity threats in today's digital landscape. One prevalent method is **Phishing**, a form of social engineering where attackers use deceptive emails, websites, or messages to trick individuals into divulging sensitive information such as login credentials, financial details, or personal information. To mitigate phishing attacks, organizations can implement email filtering solutions and conduct regular security awareness training to educate users about recognizing suspicious emails and avoiding phishing attempts. Additionally, tools like **phishery** can be used to craft convincing phishing emails and assess the effectiveness of phishing awareness programs by simulating real-world phishing scenarios within controlled environments.

Another common method of cyber attack is **Malware**, malicious software designed to infiltrate systems, steal data, or cause harm to computer networks. Examples of malware include **Viruses**, which attach themselves to legitimate programs and replicate when executed, and **Trojans**, which masquerade as legitimate software to trick users into installing them and granting unauthorized access to systems. Deploying antivirus software like **ClamAV** or **Windows Defender** can help detect and quarantine malware infections, while command-line tools like `malware-scanner` can be used to perform deep scans of file systems and directories for known malware signatures.

Ransomware represents another pervasive method of cyber attack, wherein attackers encrypt victims' data and demand ransom payments in exchange for decryption keys, effectively holding data hostage until demands are met. Mitigating the impact of ransomware attacks requires organizations to maintain up-to-date backups of critical data stored in secure, offline locations, allowing for recovery without paying ransom. Tools like **WannaCryDecryptor** can sometimes decrypt files encrypted by specific ransomware variants, provided decryption keys are publicly available or recovered through forensic analysis.

Denial-of-Service (DoS) and **Distributed Denial-of-Service (DDoS)** attacks constitute another category of cyber attack aimed at disrupting service availability by overwhelming target systems with excessive traffic or requests. Attackers may utilize botnets—networks of compromised devices—to orchestrate large-scale DDoS attacks capable of causing downtime and financial losses for organizations. Mitigating these attacks involves implementing network traffic monitoring solutions such as **tcpdump** or **Wireshark** to detect anomalous traffic patterns indicative of DoS or DDoS attacks and deploying firewall rules or **iptables** commands to block malicious traffic sources.

Man-in-the-Middle (MitM) attacks represent a stealthy method of intercepting and altering communications between parties, allowing attackers to eavesdrop on sensitive information or inject malicious content into data transmissions. Techniques like **ARP spoofing** or **DNS spoofing** can be employed to redirect traffic through attacker-controlled systems, enabling interception of plaintext passwords or session cookies transmitted over unsecured networks. To mitigate MitM attacks, organizations can implement cryptographic protocols such as **TLS** (Transport Layer Security) for encrypting communications and monitoring network traffic for signs of unauthorized interception using tools like **ettercap** or **dsniff**.

SQL Injection attacks exploit vulnerabilities in web applications' database queries, allowing attackers to manipulate SQL commands and gain unauthorized access to databases containing sensitive information. Preventing SQL Injection involves implementing secure coding practices such as parameterized queries or prepared statements to sanitize user input and prevent malicious SQL code execution. Command-line tools like **sqlmap** can automate the detection and exploitation of SQL Injection vulnerabilities in web applications, facilitating penetration testing and vulnerability assessments to identify and remediate potential security flaws.

Cross-Site Scripting (XSS) attacks represent another common method of exploiting web application vulnerabilities, wherein attackers inject malicious scripts into web pages viewed by other users. These scripts can execute arbitrary code in victims' browsers, steal session cookies, or redirect users to malicious websites controlled by attackers. Mitigating XSS attacks involves implementing input validation and output encoding techniques in web application development to sanitize user-supplied data and prevent script injection. Tools like **XSStrike** can be used to identify and exploit XSS vulnerabilities during penetration testing, helping developers secure web applications against potential attacks.

Social Engineering techniques exploit human psychology to manipulate individuals into divulging confidential information or performing actions that compromise security. Attackers may impersonate trusted entities, such as IT support personnel or senior executives, to deceive victims into disclosing passwords or granting unauthorized access to sensitive systems. Mitigating social engineering attacks requires comprehensive security awareness training for employees, emphasizing the importance of verifying requests for sensitive information or access privileges before complying. Additionally, conducting simulated phishing exercises using tools like **Gophish** can assess employees' susceptibility to social engineering tactics and reinforce best practices for recognizing and responding to suspicious requests.

In summary, understanding the diverse methods employed by cyber attackers underscores the importance of implementing robust cybersecurity measures, fostering a proactive defense posture, and continuously monitoring for emerging threats. By leveraging tools and techniques such as malware detection software, network monitoring tools, and secure coding practices, organizations can strengthen their resilience against cyber threats and safeguard sensitive data, systems, and operations from malicious actors seeking to exploit vulnerabilities in today's interconnected digital ecosystem.

Chapter 3: Basics of Digital Forensics

File System Forensics is a specialized field within digital forensics that focuses on extracting, preserving, and analyzing digital evidence from file systems to investigate cyber incidents, criminal activities, or data breaches. At its core, file system forensics involves the systematic examination of file metadata, directory structures, and allocated data blocks to reconstruct events and uncover traces of malicious activity. One fundamental aspect of file system forensics is the ability to retrieve deleted files or remnants of data that may hold critical clues for investigators. Tools such as `Autopsy` and `Sleuth Kit` are commonly used to perform disk imaging and file system analysis, capturing an exact replica of a storage device's contents and allowing forensic analysts to explore data without altering original evidence.

The process of file system forensics begins with acquisition, where forensic experts create a forensic image of a storage device using tools like `dd` (disk dump) command in Linux or `dcfldd` which is an enhanced version of `dd` that includes features such as hashing and progress indicators. This bit-by-bit copy ensures data integrity and preserves the original state of the evidence for analysis. Once acquired, the forensic image is mounted using tools like `mount` command in Linux or `FTK Imager` in Windows, allowing analysts to access and examine file system structures, directories, and individual files contained within the image.

File system forensics relies heavily on the interpretation of file system metadata, which includes information such as file timestamps (creation, modification, and access times), file size, permissions, and file allocation details. These metadata attributes provide valuable insights into the timeline of events surrounding a cyber incident or criminal activity. For instance, analyzing file timestamps can help determine when files were created, modified, or deleted, aiding investigators in reconstructing the sequence of actions taken by perpetrators. Command-line tools like `ls -l` in Linux or `dir` in Windows display file metadata attributes, allowing forensic analysts to identify anomalies or suspicious patterns indicative of unauthorized access or data manipulation.

In addition to metadata analysis, file system forensics involves examining file content to extract meaningful information and identify potential evidence of wrongdoing. Techniques such as file carving or data carving are used to recover fragmented or deleted files from unallocated disk space, where remnants of files may still exist even after deletion. Tools like `foremost` or `scalpel` are command-line utilities capable of performing file carving based on predefined file headers, footers, or file signatures, enabling forensic analysts to reconstruct deleted documents, images, or other digital artifacts crucial to an investigation.

An essential aspect of file system forensics is maintaining chain of custody and ensuring forensic soundness throughout the investigation process. Chain of custody refers to the chronological documentation of evidence handling, custody, and transfer from the initial seizure to its presentation in court, ensuring that evidence is admissible and has not been tampered with. Forensic experts use cryptographic hashing algorithms such as MD5, SHA-1, or SHA-256 with tools like `md5sum` or `sha256sum` to calculate hash values of forensic images or individual files. These hash values serve as digital fingerprints, allowing investigators to verify the integrity of evidence and detect any unauthorized modifications or alterations.

File system forensics also encompasses the analysis of file system artifacts, which are residual traces left behind by user activities and system operations within a file system. These artifacts include but are not limited to, log files, registry entries, temporary files, and system logs, providing valuable forensic artifacts that can reveal user actions, application usage patterns, and system events. Command-line tools such as `grep`, `awk`, or `find` are often used to search and analyze log files for specific keywords, timestamps, or IP addresses associated with suspicious activities or unauthorized access attempts.

Furthermore, file system forensics plays a crucial role in incident response and cybersecurity investigations, where rapid detection and analysis of file system artifacts are essential for mitigating ongoing threats and minimizing the impact of security breaches. Incident responders leverage file system forensics techniques to identify indicators of compromise (IOCs) and perform root cause analysis (RCA) to determine how an incident occurred, what systems or data were affected, and the extent of the damage. By analyzing file system metadata, file content, and system artifacts, forensic analysts can attribute malicious activities to specific threat actors, develop remediation strategies, and strengthen defenses against future cyber threats.

In summary, file system forensics is a vital discipline within digital forensics, enabling investigators to uncover evidence, reconstruct events, and support legal proceedings through the systematic examination of file system structures, metadata, and artifacts. By leveraging command-line tools, forensic analysts can acquire forensic images, analyze file system metadata, and recover deleted or fragmented files critical to investigations. As cyber threats continue to evolve, the importance of file system forensics in detecting, responding to, and mitigating cyber incidents remains paramount in safeguarding digital assets, preserving data integrity, and upholding accountability in the digital age. Basics of memory forensics encompass a critical aspect of digital forensics focused on analyzing volatile memory (RAM) to retrieve valuable information and uncover evidence of malicious activities, cyberattacks, or system compromises. Memory forensics plays a pivotal role in investigations where traditional disk-based forensics may not capture transient data or activities that reside solely in memory. The process begins with the acquisition of a memory dump, capturing the current state of RAM using tools like `LiME` (Linux Memory Extractor) or `WinPmem` in Windows, which create a forensic image of volatile memory suitable for subsequent analysis. This acquisition must be conducted carefully to avoid altering or contaminating memory contents, ensuring forensic soundness and the admissibility of evidence in legal proceedings.

Once acquired, the memory dump is analyzed using specialized tools and techniques to extract artifacts such as running processes, network connections, open files, and registry keys from memory. Tools like `Volatility` or `Rekall` (now merged into the Volatility Foundation) are widely used in memory forensics for parsing memory dumps and generating detailed reports of system activities. For instance, the `volatility pslist` command displays a list of running processes extracted from memory, including process IDs, parent process IDs, and executable paths, providing insights into active applications and potentially malicious processes.

Memory forensics enables investigators to reconstruct the sequence of events leading up to and during a security incident by analyzing memory-resident artifacts such as process memory, DLLs (Dynamic Link Libraries), and loaded drivers. DLLs loaded into process memory can be analyzed using tools like `volatility dlllist`, which enumerates DLLs loaded into each process's address space, highlighting potentially malicious libraries or injected code. This analysis helps identify indicators of compromise (IOCs) and establish a timeline of adversary actions within the compromised system.

Moreover, memory forensics is instrumental in identifying and analyzing malware residing in memory, such as rootkits or fileless malware that operate entirely in volatile memory to evade traditional detection methods. Techniques like `volatility malfind` scan memory for suspicious memory regions indicative of process injection or code injection attacks, allowing forensic analysts to identify hidden processes or malicious payloads injected into legitimate processes. By examining memory dumps with these techniques, investigators can detect stealthy malware infections, understand their behaviors, and develop effective mitigation strategies to eradicate threats.

Network forensics is another area where memory forensics provides valuable insights by analyzing network-related artifacts stored in memory, such as active network connections, socket information, and packet buffers. Commands like `volatility netscan` can be used to enumerate network connections and extract IP addresses, ports, and connection states from memory dumps, aiding in the identification of communication channels established by attackers for command-and-control (C2) activities or data exfiltration. This analysis is crucial for understanding the scope of network-based attacks and tracing malicious traffic patterns back to their origins.

In addition to malware and network artifacts, memory forensics extends to recovering user activity traces stored in volatile memory, such as user credentials, clipboard contents, and browsing history. Techniques like `volatility clipboard` examine memory for plaintext passwords or sensitive data copied to the clipboard by users, providing insights into credential theft or unauthorized data access attempts. Similarly, commands like `volatility chrome` analyze memory for artifacts associated with web browsers, including visited URLs, cookies, and cached web pages, which can reveal user activities or interactions with malicious websites.

Memory forensics also plays a crucial role in incident response scenarios, enabling rapid triage and live response capabilities to assess compromised systems' operational state and mitigate ongoing threats. Tools like `Responder` allow incident responders to analyze memory dumps in real-time, identify malicious processes or indicators of compromise, and take immediate action to contain and remediate security incidents. By leveraging memory forensics techniques during incident response, organizations can minimize downtime, mitigate data breaches, and preserve forensic evidence critical to investigations.

Furthermore, memory forensics is indispensable in forensic investigations involving advanced persistent threats (APTs) or sophisticated cyberattacks targeting high-value assets and organizations' sensitive data. APT groups often employ memory-resident malware and advanced evasion techniques to evade detection and maintain persistence within compromised systems. Memory forensics techniques such as memory analysis of malicious process memory dumps or examining process hollowing techniques used by APTs to conceal malicious activities in legitimate processes are essential for identifying and neutralizing persistent threats.

Legal and regulatory compliance considerations are paramount in memory forensics, requiring adherence to established procedures, chain of custody protocols, and privacy regulations governing the handling and analysis of volatile memory dumps. Forensic analysts must document their methodologies, findings, and forensic procedures to ensure the admissibility and integrity of evidence in legal proceedings. Additionally, encryption and hashing techniques like `md5sum` or `sha256sum` are applied to memory dumps to verify their integrity and prevent unauthorized tampering or alteration, safeguarding the forensic integrity of volatile memory analysis.

In summary, memory forensics represents a critical discipline within digital forensics, providing investigators with the capability to extract, analyze, and interpret volatile memory artifacts to uncover evidence of cyber incidents, malware infections, and malicious activities. By leveraging command-line tools and advanced techniques, forensic analysts can conduct comprehensive memory analysis, identify indicators of compromise, and support incident response efforts to mitigate cyber threats effectively. As cyber adversaries continue to evolve their tactics, memory forensics remains essential in enhancing cybersecurity resilience, preserving data integrity, and enabling organizations to respond proactively to emerging threats in an increasingly interconnected digital landscape.

Chapter 4: Principles of Counterintelligence in Cybersecurity

The role of counterintelligence in proactive defense is pivotal within cybersecurity strategies, focusing on identifying, mitigating, and neutralizing threats posed by malicious actors, espionage activities, and insider threats before they can inflict harm or compromise organizational security. Counterintelligence operates on the premise of understanding adversaries' tactics, techniques, and motivations to preemptively detect and disrupt their operations, safeguarding sensitive information, intellectual property, and critical infrastructure from espionage or cyberattacks. Central to proactive defense is the deployment of advanced threat detection and intelligence gathering techniques, such as **OSINT** (Open Source Intelligence), which involves collecting and analyzing publicly available information from websites, social media platforms, or online forums frequented by threat actors to gather insights into their activities and intentions. Tools like `theHarvester` or `Maltego` facilitate OSINT operations by automating the retrieval and correlation of information related to potential adversaries, enabling cybersecurity teams to anticipate and mitigate emerging threats effectively.

Counterintelligence also encompasses **HUMINT** (Human Intelligence), involving the collection and analysis of intelligence gathered from human sources such as informants, insiders, or personnel with access to sensitive information. HUMINT operations within organizations rely on cultivating trusted relationships, conducting interviews, or eliciting information from employees to identify potential insider threats, unauthorized disclosures of information, or vulnerabilities that could be exploited by adversaries. Techniques such as conducting security interviews using structured questionnaires or psychological assessments can help assess individuals' trustworthiness and identify indicators of suspicious behavior or unauthorized activities.

In addition to human intelligence, **SIGINT** (Signals Intelligence) plays a crucial role in counterintelligence by intercepting and analyzing electronic communications, radio signals, or telecommunications data to gather intelligence on adversaries' activities or potential cyber threats. SIGINT techniques involve deploying monitoring tools like `Wireshark` or `tcpdump` to capture and analyze network traffic for anomalous patterns indicative of unauthorized access attempts, data exfiltration, or reconnaissance activities conducted by threat actors. By monitoring and analyzing SIGINT, cybersecurity teams can detect and respond promptly to malicious activities before they escalate into security incidents or breaches.

Moreover, proactive defense through counterintelligence emphasizes the importance of **Insider Threat Detection**, focusing on identifying and mitigating risks posed by trusted insiders who may inadvertently or maliciously compromise organizational security. Techniques such as **User Behavior Analytics (UBA)** leverage machine learning algorithms and statistical analysis to detect deviations from normal user behavior, anomalous activities, or access patterns indicative of insider threats. Tools like `Splunk Enterprise Security` or `UEBA (User and Entity Behavior Analytics)` platforms aggregate and correlate data from multiple sources, including logs, endpoint telemetry, and network traffic, to identify insider threats and potential indicators of compromised accounts or privileged access abuse within the organization.

Furthermore, proactive defense strategies include **Vulnerability Management**, which involves identifying, prioritizing, and remediating security vulnerabilities within systems, applications, or infrastructure before they can be exploited by adversaries. Vulnerability scanning tools like `Nessus`, `OpenVAS`, or `Qualys` automate the discovery and assessment of vulnerabilities across networks, servers, and endpoints, generating reports that highlight critical vulnerabilities requiring immediate patching or mitigation measures. By addressing vulnerabilities proactively, organizations can reduce the attack surface, strengthen defenses against exploitation, and mitigate the risk of cyber incidents or data breaches resulting from known security weaknesses.

Another essential component of counterintelligence in proactive defense is **Threat Hunting**, a proactive approach to identifying and neutralizing advanced threats or persistent adversaries operating within organizational networks. Threat hunting involves leveraging threat intelligence feeds, behavioral analytics, and heuristic detection techniques to search for signs of compromise, unauthorized activities, or indicators of malicious behavior that may evade traditional security controls. Tools like `Carbon Black`, `CrowdStrike Falcon`, or `Elastic Security` provide capabilities for real-time monitoring, threat detection, and incident response, enabling cybersecurity teams to conduct proactive threat hunting operations and respond swiftly to emerging threats before they can escalate into significant security incidents.

Additionally, **Deception Technologies** play a crucial role in proactive defense by deploying decoy systems, files, or credentials designed to lure and deceive adversaries attempting to infiltrate or compromise organizational networks. Deception techniques such as **Honeypots** simulate vulnerable systems or services within a network to attract and divert attackers away from critical assets, providing cybersecurity teams with valuable insights into adversaries' tactics, techniques, and objectives. Tools like `KFSensor` or `Cymulate` enable organizations to deploy and manage deception environments effectively, monitoring adversary interactions and gathering intelligence on emerging threats to enhance defensive strategies.

Furthermore, proactive defense strategies encompass **Incident Response Planning and Preparedness**, emphasizing the development of comprehensive incident response plans, playbooks, and tabletop exercises to ensure organizations are well-equipped to detect, contain, and mitigate security incidents promptly. Incident response frameworks such as **NIST SP 800-61** provide guidelines for establishing incident response capabilities, defining roles and responsibilities, and establishing communication protocols to coordinate response efforts during cyber incidents. Command-line tools like `MISP` (Malware Information Sharing Platform) facilitate information sharing and collaboration among incident response teams, enabling swift coordination and response to mitigate the impact of security breaches or cyberattacks.

In summary, the role of counterintelligence in proactive defense is essential for organizations seeking to strengthen their cybersecurity posture, mitigate emerging threats, and protect sensitive assets from espionage, cyber espionage, or insider threats. By integrating advanced threat detection techniques, intelligence gathering capabilities, and proactive defense strategies such as vulnerability management, threat hunting, and deception technologies, organizations can enhance their resilience against evolving cyber threats and maintain operational continuity in an increasingly complex threat landscape. Counterintelligence techniques and tools are critical components of cybersecurity strategies aimed at identifying, mitigating, and countering threats posed by malicious actors, insiders, or adversaries seeking to compromise organizational security or exploit vulnerabilities for illicit gain. These techniques encompass a wide range of proactive and defensive measures designed to detect, deter, and disrupt espionage activities, cyberattacks, or unauthorized access attempts within networks, systems, or sensitive data repositories. One fundamental counterintelligence technique is **OSINT** (Open Source Intelligence), which involves collecting and analyzing publicly available information from websites, social media platforms, or online forums frequented by threat actors to gather insights into their activities and intentions. Tools like `theHarvester` or `Maltego` automate OSINT operations, facilitating the retrieval and correlation of information related to potential adversaries and their affiliations, aiding in threat assessment and intelligence gathering efforts.

Counterintelligence efforts also encompass **HUMINT** (Human Intelligence), leveraging human sources such as informants, insiders, or individuals with access to sensitive information to gather actionable intelligence on threats or malicious activities targeting organizational assets. HUMINT techniques involve conducting interviews, eliciting information through interpersonal interactions, or leveraging psychological assessments to identify insider threats, assess employee trustworthiness, and detect potential vulnerabilities susceptible to exploitation. Techniques such as structured security interviews or behavioral analysis are employed to assess individuals' motives, behaviors, and intentions, providing insights into insider threats or unauthorized disclosures that could compromise organizational security.

In addition to human intelligence, **SIGINT** (Signals Intelligence) plays a crucial role in counterintelligence by intercepting and analyzing electronic communications, radio signals, or telecommunications data to gather intelligence on adversaries' activities or potential cyber threats. SIGINT techniques involve deploying monitoring tools such as `Wireshark` or `tcpdump` to capture and analyze network traffic for anomalous patterns indicative of unauthorized access attempts, data exfiltration, or reconnaissance activities conducted by threat actors. By monitoring and analyzing SIGINT, cybersecurity teams can detect and respond promptly to malicious activities before they escalate into security incidents or breaches.

Moreover, counterintelligence techniques include **Counter Surveillance**, aimed at identifying and mitigating physical or technical surveillance attempts targeting organizational assets, facilities, or personnel. Physical counter-surveillance involves conducting physical sweeps, monitoring surveillance detection zones, or employing technical surveillance countermeasures (TSCM) to detect and neutralize covert surveillance devices such as hidden cameras, audio bugs, or GPS trackers. Techniques like RF spectrum analysis or infrared thermal imaging are used to detect electromagnetic emissions or anomalies indicative of electronic surveillance devices, safeguarding sensitive conversations or operational activities from unauthorized monitoring.

Furthermore, **Deception Technologies** play a crucial role in counterintelligence by deploying decoy systems, files, or credentials designed to lure and deceive adversaries attempting to infiltrate or compromise organizational networks. Deception techniques such as **Honeypots** simulate vulnerable systems or services within a network to attract and divert attackers away from critical assets, providing cybersecurity teams with valuable insights into adversaries' tactics, techniques, and objectives. Tools like `KFSensor` or `Cymulate` enable organizations to deploy and manage deception environments effectively, monitoring adversary interactions and gathering intelligence on emerging threats to enhance defensive strategies.

In addition to proactive measures, counterintelligence involves **Insider Threat Detection**, focusing on identifying and mitigating risks posed by trusted insiders who may inadvertently or maliciously compromise organizational security. Techniques such as **User Behavior Analytics (UBA)** leverage machine learning algorithms and statistical analysis to detect deviations from normal user behavior, anomalous activities, or access patterns indicative of insider threats. Tools like

`Splunk Enterprise Security` or `UEBA (User and Entity Behavior Analytics)` platforms aggregate and correlate data from multiple sources, including logs, endpoint telemetry, and network traffic, to identify insider threats and potential indicators of compromised accounts or privileged access abuse within the organization.

Moreover, counterintelligence efforts encompass **Vulnerability Management**, which involves identifying, prioritizing, and remediating security vulnerabilities within systems, applications, or infrastructure before they can be exploited by adversaries. Vulnerability scanning tools like `Nessus`, `OpenVAS`, or `Qualys` automate the discovery and assessment of vulnerabilities across networks, servers, and endpoints, generating reports that highlight critical vulnerabilities requiring immediate patching or mitigation measures. By addressing vulnerabilities proactively, organizations can reduce the attack surface, strengthen defenses against exploitation, and mitigate the risk of cyber incidents or data breaches resulting from known security weaknesses.

Additionally, **Threat Intelligence Sharing** plays a crucial role in counterintelligence by facilitating collaboration and information exchange among organizations, government agencies, and cybersecurity communities to identify emerging threats, tactics, and adversary behaviors. Threat intelligence platforms such as `MISP` (Malware Information Sharing Platform) enable organizations to share actionable threat intelligence, indicators of compromise (IOCs), and contextual information on cyber threats in real-time, enhancing situational awareness and enabling proactive defense measures against evolving threats.

In summary, counterintelligence techniques and tools are essential components of comprehensive cybersecurity strategies, enabling organizations to detect, deter, and mitigate threats posed by malicious actors, insiders, or adversaries seeking to exploit vulnerabilities for illicit purposes. By integrating OSINT, HUMINT, SIGINT, and other advanced techniques into proactive defense measures such as deception technologies, insider threat detection, vulnerability management, and threat intelligence sharing, organizations can enhance their resilience against evolving cyber threats and safeguard sensitive assets from espionage, cyber espionage, or unauthorized access attempts in today's dynamic threat landscape.

Chapter 5: Incident Detection and Initial Response

Techniques for real-time incident detection are crucial in cybersecurity operations, enabling organizations to identify and respond swiftly to security breaches, unauthorized access attempts, or malicious activities targeting their networks, systems, or data repositories. One fundamental technique is **Log Analysis**, which involves monitoring and analyzing log files generated by operating systems, applications, network devices, and security tools to detect abnormal behaviors or indicators of compromise (IOCs) that may signify a security incident. Commands like `grep` in Unix-based systems or `Select-String` in PowerShell are used to search log files for specific keywords, IP addresses, or error codes associated with suspicious activities, providing insights into potential security incidents requiring further investigation.

Another essential technique for real-time incident detection is **Network Traffic Analysis**, which involves capturing, inspecting, and analyzing network packets to identify anomalies, unauthorized communications, or malicious traffic indicative of cyberattacks. Tools like `Wireshark` or `tcpdump` are used to capture network traffic on specific interfaces or subnets, allowing cybersecurity teams to analyze packet headers, payloads, and protocol behavior to detect signs of reconnaissance, data exfiltration, or command-and-control (C2) communications. Techniques such as

`Wireshark -r <pcap_file>` enable offline analysis of packet captures, while live monitoring with `tcpdump -i eth0` facilitates real-time traffic inspection for suspicious patterns or anomalies.

Furthermore, **Endpoint Detection and Response (EDR)** solutions play a crucial role in real-time incident detection by continuously monitoring endpoint devices such as workstations, servers, or mobile devices for signs of malicious activity, unauthorized access, or system compromises. EDR tools like `CrowdStrike Falcon`, `Carbon Black`, or `Microsoft Defender for Endpoint` utilize endpoint telemetry, behavior-based analytics, and machine learning algorithms to detect and respond to suspicious activities, fileless malware, or advanced persistent threats (APTs) that evade traditional antivirus defenses. Commands such as `edrctl query incidents` or `edrcli search -query "suspicious behavior"` enable security analysts to query EDR platforms for incident alerts or behavioral anomalies requiring immediate investigation and remediation.

Moreover, **Behavioral Analysis** techniques involve monitoring and analyzing user and system behaviors to detect deviations from normal patterns or activities that may indicate unauthorized access, insider threats, or malware infections. Behavioral analysis tools like `Splunk Enterprise Security` or `UEBA (User and Entity Behavior Analytics)` platforms leverage machine learning algorithms and statistical models to establish baselines of normal behavior and identify anomalies, such as unusual file access patterns, privilege escalation attempts, or login anomalies that may signify a security incident. Commands like `splunk search "index=main host=webserver1"` query log data to detect suspicious activities or behavioral deviations indicative of potential security threats.

Additionally, **Threat Intelligence Integration** enhances real-time incident detection by integrating external threat intelligence feeds, indicators of compromise (IOCs), or contextual information on known threats into security monitoring and alerting systems. Threat intelligence platforms like `MISP` (Malware Information Sharing Platform) enable organizations to ingest and correlate threat intelligence data, enriching security alerts with additional context, such as threat actor tactics, techniques, and procedures (TTPs), to prioritize incident response efforts and mitigate emerging threats effectively. Commands such as `misp-galaxy search "APT28"` query threat intelligence repositories for information on specific threat actors or campaigns associated with recent cyber incidents, enhancing situational awareness and proactive defense measures.

Furthermore, **File Integrity Monitoring (FIM)** is essential for real-time incident detection by continuously monitoring changes to critical system files, configurations, or directories for unauthorized modifications, file deletions, or tampering indicative of a security breach or insider threat. FIM tools like `Tripwire`, `AIDE (Advanced Intrusion Detection Environment)`, or built-in features like `auditd` in Linux systems audit file access and modifications, generating alerts or notifications when unauthorized changes are detected. Commands such as `auditctl -w /etc/passwd -p wa` configure file auditing rules to monitor specific files or directories for changes, while `aide --check` verifies file integrity based on predefined baseline configurations, enabling security teams to detect and respond promptly to unauthorized modifications or system compromises.

Moreover, **Anomaly Detection** techniques leverage machine learning algorithms, statistical analysis, or heuristics to identify abnormal behaviors, events, or patterns that deviate from expected norms within network traffic, user activities, or system operations. Anomaly detection tools and platforms like `ELK Stack (Elasticsearch, Logstash, Kibana)` or `Azure Sentinel` analyze vast amounts of telemetry data, logs, or security events to detect outliers, unusual spikes in network traffic, or unusual user behaviors indicative of potential security incidents. Commands such as `kibana dashboard` in ELK Stack or `az sentinel query` in Azure Sentinel enable security analysts to visualize and query anomaly detection results, facilitating early detection and response to emerging threats before they escalate into significant security incidents.

In summary, techniques for real-time incident detection are essential for organizations seeking to enhance their cybersecurity posture, detect threats promptly, and mitigate the impact of security breaches or unauthorized access attempts. By leveraging log analysis, network traffic analysis, endpoint detection and response (EDR), behavioral analysis, threat intelligence integration, file integrity monitoring (FIM), and anomaly detection techniques, cybersecurity teams can monitor, analyze, and respond effectively to security incidents in real-time, minimizing potential damage, preserving data integrity, and safeguarding organizational assets against evolving cyber threats. Immediate actions for incident containment are critical in cybersecurity operations, as they involve swift and decisive measures to mitigate the impact of security breaches, limit unauthorized access, and prevent further compromise of organizational assets, data, or infrastructure. One of the primary immediate actions is **Isolation of Compromised Systems**, which involves disconnecting affected systems or endpoints from the network to prevent malicious actors from accessing additional resources, spreading malware, or conducting further unauthorized activities. Commands such as `ifconfig eth0 down` in Linux or `Disable-NetAdapter -Name "Ethernet"` in PowerShell disable network interfaces or adapters, isolating compromised systems while allowing forensic analysts to conduct investigations without interference.

Another essential immediate action for incident containment is **Changing Compromised Credentials**, which entails resetting passwords, revoking compromised credentials, or disabling compromised accounts to prevent unauthorized access to sensitive data or systems. Commands like `passwd username` in Linux or `Set-ADAccountPassword -Identity username -Reset -NewPassword (ConvertTo-SecureString -AsPlainText "newPassword" -Force)` in PowerShell enable administrators to change user passwords securely, ensuring that compromised credentials no longer provide access to organizational resources or privileged accounts susceptible to exploitation.

Moreover, **Patch and Vulnerability Management** is crucial for incident containment by promptly applying security patches, updates, or hotfixes to vulnerable systems, applications, or services identified during incident response activities. Vulnerability scanning tools such as `Nessus`, `OpenVAS`, or `Qualys` automate the discovery of vulnerabilities, generating reports that highlight critical security issues requiring immediate remediation. Commands such as `yum update` in CentOS or `apt-get upgrade` in Ubuntu initiate the installation of available updates and patches, closing security gaps and reducing the risk of exploitation by threat actors targeting known vulnerabilities.

Additionally, **Deploying Firewall Rules and Access Controls** is essential for incident containment to restrict unauthorized network traffic, block malicious IP addresses, or implement segmentation to contain the impact of security incidents and prevent lateral movement within organizational networks. Firewall management commands like `iptables` in Linux or `New-NetFirewallRule` in PowerShell enable administrators to create and enforce firewall rules that limit inbound and outbound traffic, mitigate distributed denial-of-service (DDoS) attacks, or block communication with known malicious domains or IP addresses identified during incident response activities.

Furthermore, **Implementing Intrusion Prevention Systems (IPS)** facilitates incident containment by deploying proactive measures to detect and block malicious activities, exploit attempts, or unauthorized system modifications in real-time. IPS solutions like `Snort`, `Suricata`, or `Cisco Firepower` monitor network traffic for suspicious patterns or signatures indicative of known threats, triggering automated responses such as blocking malicious IP addresses or quarantining compromised endpoints. Commands such as `snort -c /etc/snort/snort.conf -i eth0 -A console` initialize Snort with specific configuration files and network interfaces, enabling real-time intrusion detection and prevention capabilities to mitigate ongoing security incidents effectively.

Moreover, **Data Backup and Recovery** is essential for incident containment to ensure data integrity, availability, and resilience against ransomware attacks, data breaches, or system compromises. Backup solutions such as `rsync` in Linux or `robocopy` in Windows facilitate data replication to secure off-site locations or cloud storage platforms, enabling organizations to restore critical data and systems in the event of data loss or corruption caused by security incidents. Commands like `rsync -av /path/to/source /path/to/destination` synchronize data between source and destination directories, while `robocopy /MIR /SEC /COPYALL` in Windows replicates files and directory structures while preserving file permissions and attributes.

Additionally, **Implementing Incident Response Playbooks** facilitates incident containment by defining predefined workflows, escalation procedures, and response actions tailored to specific types of security incidents or threat scenarios. Incident response platforms such as `TheHive`, `Splunk Enterprise Security`, or `IBM Resilient` automate incident triage, orchestration, and response coordination, enabling security teams to execute containment actions promptly and effectively. Commands such as `resilient-circuits execute "incident_id" -action playbookAction` in IBM Resilient trigger automated response actions based on incident response playbooks, streamlining incident containment efforts and ensuring consistent response procedures across organizational security operations.

Furthermore, **Forensic Evidence Preservation** is crucial for incident containment to maintain the integrity and admissibility of digital evidence required for post-incident analysis, legal proceedings, or regulatory compliance. Forensic imaging tools such as `dd` in Linux or `FTK Imager` in Windows create bit-by-bit copies of storage devices, preserving volatile memory or disk contents without altering original data. Commands such as `dd if=/dev/sda of=image.dd bs=1M` capture disk images for forensic analysis, while `ftkimager.exe acquire --out image.e01` in FTK Imager acquires forensic images in Encase format, ensuring forensic integrity and chain of custody during incident response investigations.

In summary, immediate actions for incident containment are essential for organizations to minimize the impact of security breaches, mitigate ongoing threats, and restore operational continuity swiftly. By isolating compromised systems, changing compromised credentials, applying patches and updates, deploying firewall rules and access controls, implementing intrusion prevention systems, backing up critical data, executing incident response playbooks, and preserving forensic evidence, cybersecurity teams can effectively contain security incidents, reduce potential damage, and enhance resilience against evolving cyber threats in today's dynamic threat landscape.

Chapter 6: Collecting and Preserving Digital Evidence

Best practices for evidence collection in cybersecurity are essential for ensuring the integrity, admissibility, and usefulness of digital evidence during incident response, forensic investigations, or legal proceedings. One fundamental practice is **Chain of Custody Documentation**, which involves maintaining detailed records documenting the handling, storage, and transfer of digital evidence from the initial collection phase through analysis and presentation in court. Tools like `Evidence Tracker` or `Chain of Custody Software` automate chain of custody documentation, recording timestamps, custodians, and activities associated with evidence handling to establish accountability and preserve the evidentiary value of collected data.

Another critical best practice is **Forensic Imaging**, which entails creating forensically sound copies or images of storage devices such as hard drives, solid-state drives (SSDs), or mobile devices to preserve volatile memory or disk contents without altering original data. Forensic imaging tools like `dd`, `dcfldd`, or `FTK Imager` in Linux and Windows environments facilitate bit-by-bit imaging of storage media, ensuring data integrity and enabling forensic analysts to conduct offline analysis or data recovery procedures. Commands such as `dd if=/dev/sda of=image.dd bs=1M` in Linux or `ftkimager.exe acquire --out image.e01` in FTK Imager create forensic images in Encase format, preserving evidence for subsequent forensic examination.

Moreover, **Documentation of Collection Methods and Procedures** is crucial for evidence integrity, requiring detailed documentation of collection methods, techniques, and tools used during digital evidence acquisition. Documentation should include timestamps, system configurations, and environmental conditions at the time of evidence collection to provide context and establish the reliability of collected data in forensic analysis or legal proceedings. Techniques such as **Hash Verification** validate the integrity of forensic images or acquired data by generating cryptographic hash values such as MD5, SHA-256, or SHA-512 to verify that evidence remains unchanged throughout the investigation process. Commands like `md5sum` or `sha256sum` in Linux calculate hash values for files or disk images, enabling forensic analysts to verify data integrity and detect tampering or alterations.

Furthermore, **Minimization of Data Alteration** is essential during evidence collection to avoid inadvertently modifying or contaminating digital evidence, ensuring its admissibility and reliability in forensic investigations or court proceedings. Forensic acquisition tools such as `Forensic Toolkit (FTK) Imager` or `EnCase Forensic` employ write-blocking mechanisms to prevent write operations to storage media during imaging, preserving original data integrity and maintaining the forensic soundness of collected evidence. Commands like `ftkimager.exe acquire -- nobadblocks` in FTK Imager disable bad block handling during forensic imaging to minimize alterations and ensure accurate preservation of digital evidence for forensic examination.

Moreover, **Documentation of Evidence Custodianship** involves assigning custodians responsible for overseeing and safeguarding digital evidence throughout the chain of custody process, maintaining records of custodian identities, responsibilities, and activities related to evidence handling. Custodians adhere to established procedures, security protocols, and legal requirements governing evidence custody to prevent unauthorized access, tampering, or loss of critical data during incident response or forensic investigations. Techniques such as **Write-Blocking** ensure data preservation and integrity by preventing write operations to storage devices during forensic imaging, preserving original data contents and minimizing the risk of data alteration or contamination during evidence collection.

Additionally, **Adherence to Legal and Regulatory Requirements** is essential for evidence collection to ensure compliance with applicable laws, regulations, and standards governing digital evidence acquisition, storage, and disclosure. Legal considerations such as chain of custody documentation, admissibility requirements, and privacy protections govern the collection, handling, and disclosure of digital evidence in criminal investigations, civil litigation, or regulatory compliance audits. Tools like `Encase Forensic`, `AccessData FTK`, or `X-Ways Forensics` support forensic imaging and analysis while maintaining compliance with legal and regulatory requirements, facilitating the extraction, preservation, and presentation of digital evidence in court.

Furthermore, **Collaboration with Legal Counsel and Stakeholders** enhances evidence collection practices by engaging legal counsel, compliance officers, or internal stakeholders early in the incident response process to ensure alignment with legal strategies, privacy considerations, and regulatory obligations. Legal professionals provide guidance on evidence preservation, data privacy, and chain of custody documentation requirements, facilitating the admissibility and reliability of digital evidence in legal proceedings. Techniques such as **Documentation of Incident Response Actions** involve documenting incident response activities, decisions, and communications to provide a comprehensive audit trail of actions taken during evidence collection, analysis, and mitigation efforts.

Moreover, **Training and Certification** of incident responders and forensic analysts in proper evidence handling techniques, legal procedures, and industry standards enhances the reliability and admissibility of digital evidence in court. Training programs such as **Certified Forensic Examiner (CFE)** or **Certified

Information Systems Security Professional (CISSP)** provide practitioners with the knowledge, skills, and certifications necessary to conduct forensic investigations, adhere to legal requirements, and maintain the integrity of collected evidence throughout the incident response lifecycle. Techniques such as **Documentation of Forensic Analysis Findings** involve documenting findings, conclusions, and recommendations derived from forensic analysis to support incident response efforts, legal proceedings, or regulatory compliance initiatives.

In summary, best practices for evidence collection in cybersecurity encompass chain of custody documentation, forensic imaging, documentation of collection methods and procedures, hash verification, minimization of data alteration, documentation of evidence custodianship, adherence to legal and regulatory requirements, collaboration with legal counsel and stakeholders, training and certification, and documentation of incident response actions. By adhering to these practices, organizations can enhance the integrity, admissibility, and reliability of digital evidence during incident response, forensic investigations, or legal proceedings, ensuring effective resolution of security incidents and safeguarding organizational assets against cyber threats in today's complex threat landscape. Chain of custody in digital forensics refers to the meticulous documentation and handling procedures that track the chronological history of digital evidence from its initial collection through analysis, storage, and presentation in legal proceedings, ensuring its integrity, authenticity, and admissibility in court. One of the primary aspects of chain of custody is **Documentation**, involving detailed records that capture essential information such as the date, time, location, and identity of individuals involved in each stage of evidence handling. Tools like **Evidence Tracker** or **Chain of Custody Software** automate the documentation process, recording timestamps, custodians, and activities associated with evidence handling to establish accountability and preserve the evidentiary value of collected data.

Additionally, **Secure Storage** plays a crucial role in maintaining chain of custody by ensuring that digital evidence is stored in a controlled environment that safeguards against unauthorized access, tampering, or alteration. Secure storage facilities, evidence lockers, or digital evidence management systems employ access controls, encryption, and audit logging to protect sensitive data from compromise during storage. Techniques such as **Encryption** using tools like **BitLocker** or **VeraCrypt** ensure data confidentiality and integrity, preventing unauthorized access to digital evidence while in storage and enhancing compliance with privacy regulations and legal requirements.

Moreover, **Physical Security Controls** are essential for maintaining chain of custody integrity by implementing measures such as surveillance cameras, access control systems, and tamper-evident seals to monitor and protect physical access to digital evidence storage areas. Physical security protocols and procedures restrict access to authorized personnel only, reducing the risk of evidence tampering or theft and ensuring the reliability of evidence presented in court. Techniques such as **Tamper-Evident Packaging** seal evidence containers or storage media with unique identifiers or security seals to detect unauthorized access attempts and validate the integrity of digital evidence during transit or storage.

Furthermore, **Digital Evidence Seizure** involves the lawful acquisition and removal of digital evidence from its original location, ensuring compliance with legal procedures, search warrants, or consent requirements governing evidence collection in criminal investigations or litigation. Forensic imaging tools like **dd**, **dcfldd**, or **FTK Imager** create forensically sound copies of storage devices, preserving volatile memory or disk contents without altering original data during evidence seizure. Commands such as `dd if=/dev/sda of=image.dd bs=1M` in Linux or `ftkimager.exe acquire --out image.e01` in FTK Imager facilitate bit-by-bit imaging of storage media, while documenting the seizure process ensures adherence to chain of custody protocols and legal standards.

Additionally, **Authentication and Verification** are critical for establishing the authenticity and reliability of digital evidence by documenting procedures that verify the accuracy, completeness, and integrity of acquired data during forensic analysis. Techniques such as **Hash Verification** calculate cryptographic hash values like **MD5**, **SHA-256**, or **SHA-512** to verify that forensic images or acquired data remain unchanged throughout the investigation process. Commands like `md5sum` or `sha256sum` in Linux calculate hash values for files or disk images, enabling forensic analysts to detect tampering, alterations, or data corruption that may affect the integrity and admissibility of digital evidence in court.

Moreover, **Handling Procedures** dictate the proper techniques and protocols for transporting, storing, and accessing digital evidence to minimize the risk of contamination, loss, or unauthorized access during chain of custody. Forensic examiners adhere to established handling procedures, security protocols, and legal guidelines to maintain the integrity and reliability of digital evidence throughout the forensic investigation lifecycle. Techniques such as **Write-Blocking** prevent write operations to storage media during forensic imaging, preserving original data contents and ensuring forensic soundness in compliance with chain of custody requirements.

Furthermore, **Legal Documentation** involves preparing and maintaining documentation that supports the admissibility of digital evidence in court, including affidavits, incident reports, forensic examination reports, and chain of custody logs detailing the acquisition, handling, and analysis of digital evidence. Legal professionals collaborate with forensic examiners to ensure that documentation meets evidentiary standards, complies with legal procedures, and supports the reliability and credibility of digital evidence presented in litigation or criminal proceedings. Techniques such as **Documentation of Custodianship** record custodians responsible for overseeing and safeguarding digital evidence throughout its lifecycle, ensuring accountability and transparency in evidence handling practices.

In summary, chain of custody in digital forensics encompasses documentation, secure storage, physical security controls, digital evidence seizure, authentication and verification, handling procedures, and legal documentation to ensure the integrity, authenticity, and admissibility of digital evidence in legal proceedings. By adhering to these best practices and techniques, forensic examiners and legal professionals can preserve the chain of custody, protect the evidentiary value of digital evidence, and support effective prosecution or defense strategies in criminal investigations, civil litigation, or regulatory compliance matters within the dynamic landscape of digital forensics.

Chapter 7: Analyzing and Interpreting Forensic Data

Methods of data recovery and reconstruction in digital forensics are essential techniques used to retrieve and reconstruct data from damaged, corrupted, deleted, or intentionally altered storage devices, enabling forensic investigators to recover crucial evidence for investigative or legal purposes. One of the fundamental methods is **File Carving**, which involves extracting fragmented or deleted files from storage media by identifying file headers, footers, and data structures indicative of specific file types such as documents, images, or videos, utilizing tools like **Scalpel**, **PhotoRec**, or **Foremost** that analyze disk images or partitions to recover lost or deleted files based on predefined file signatures or patterns.

Another critical technique is **Partition Recovery**, aimed at recovering deleted, lost, or inaccessible partitions on storage devices such as hard drives or SSDs using tools like **TestDisk**, **EaseUS Partition Recovery**, or **Disk Drill**, which scan disk sectors for traces of lost partitions, reconstruct partition tables, and restore access to data stored within recovered partitions. Commands such as `testdisk /dev/sda` can be used to initiate the partition recovery process by analyzing disk structures and recovering lost or deleted partitions based on sector information and partition table reconstructions.

Moreover, **Deleted File Recovery** focuses on recovering files that have been deleted from storage media but remain recoverable until overwritten by new data, utilizing tools like **Recuva**, **PhotoRec**, or **R-Studio** that scan disk sectors for traces of deleted files, restore file metadata, and reconstruct file contents from unallocated disk space or file system metadata. Commands such as `recuva /debug` in Windows or `photorec /dev/sda` in Linux facilitate file recovery processes by scanning disk sectors for deleted file signatures and reconstructing file structures to recover files deleted due to accidental deletion, formatting errors, or malicious actions.

Additionally, **RAID Data Reconstruction** techniques recover data from redundant array of independent disks (RAID) configurations that have experienced disk failures, corruption, or logical errors by reconstructing RAID arrays, using tools like **R-Studio Network Edition**, **UFS Explorer RAID Recovery**, or **ReclaiMe Pro** that analyze disk parity information, reconstruct RAID configurations, and recover data from failed or degraded RAID arrays. Commands such as `mdadm --assemble --run /dev/md0` in Linux or `diskpart` in Windows enable administrators to manage RAID configurations, rebuild failed arrays, and restore data integrity following RAID controller failures or disk drive malfunctions.

Furthermore, **Forensic Imaging and Data Extraction** methods involve creating forensic images or bit-by-bit copies of storage devices using tools like **dd**, **dcfldd**, or **FTK Imager** that capture complete disk images, preserving volatile memory or disk contents without altering original data during evidence acquisition. Commands such as `dd if=/dev/sda of=image.dd bs=1M` in Linux or `ftkimager.exe acquire --out image.e01` in FTK Imager facilitate forensic imaging by creating exact replicas of storage media, ensuring data integrity and enabling offline analysis or data recovery procedures to extract valuable evidence for forensic examination.

Moreover, **Database Reconstruction** techniques recover data from corrupt or damaged databases using database recovery tools like **Oracle Data Recovery**, **SQL Server Database Recovery**, or **MySQL Recovery Toolbox** that repair database structures, restore transaction logs, and recover data records from backup files or database snapshots. Commands such as `sqlplus / as sysdba` in Oracle or `mysql -u root -p` in MySQL initiate database recovery operations by accessing database management interfaces, restoring backup files, and executing database repair scripts to resolve data corruption issues and recover critical information stored within databases.

Additionally, **Email Recovery** methods retrieve deleted or inaccessible emails from email servers, client applications, or backup archives using email recovery tools like **Stellar Repair for Outlook**, **Kernel for Exchange Server**, or **DataNumen Exchange

Recovery** that scan mailbox databases, reconstruct email messages, and restore attachments from corrupted or inaccessible email storage formats. Commands such as `exmerge` in Exchange Server or `outlook.exe /resetfolders` in Microsoft Outlook initiate email recovery processes by accessing mailbox databases, exporting recovered emails, and restoring deleted items from backup archives or offline storage files.

Furthermore, **File System Reconstruction** techniques rebuild corrupted or damaged file systems on storage devices using file system repair utilities like **fsck** in Linux or **chkdsk** in Windows that scan disk sectors, repair file system metadata structures, and recover data from file system inconsistencies or errors. Commands such as `fsck /dev/sda1` in Linux or `chkdsk /f /r` in Windows initiate file system repair operations by analyzing disk partitions, correcting file system errors, and restoring access to data stored within damaged file systems caused by disk errors, power failures, or software crashes.

Moreover, **Virtual Machine Recovery** methods restore virtual machines (VMs) and virtualized environments from backup snapshots or virtual machine disk (VMDK) files using virtual machine recovery tools like **Veeam Backup & Replication**, **VMware vSphere Data Protection**, or **Acronis Cyber Backup** that restore VM configurations, virtual disks, and guest operating systems from backup repositories or cloud storage platforms. Commands such as `vmkfstools -i source.vmdk -d thin destination.vmdk` in VMware enable administrators to clone virtual disks, migrate VMs between hosts, and recover VMs from backup snapshots or virtual machine images, ensuring business continuity and data availability in virtualized IT environments.

In summary, methods of data recovery and reconstruction in digital forensics encompass file carving, partition recovery, deleted file recovery, RAID data reconstruction, forensic imaging and data extraction, database reconstruction, email recovery, file system reconstruction, and virtual machine recovery techniques that facilitate the retrieval, reconstruction, and analysis of digital evidence from various sources and platforms. By leveraging these methods and tools, forensic investigators can recover critical evidence, reconstruct digital artifacts, and support investigative or legal proceedings by preserving data integrity, ensuring evidentiary admissibility, and enabling comprehensive analysis of digital evidence in today's complex forensic investigations landscape. Interpretation of metadata in forensic analysis plays a crucial role in uncovering digital evidence and reconstructing the activities surrounding digital artifacts, providing forensic investigators with valuable insights into the creation, modification, and usage history of files, documents, emails, and other digital entities. One fundamental aspect of metadata analysis is **File Metadata Examination**, which involves scrutinizing attributes such as file creation dates, modification timestamps, file sizes, and author details embedded within file headers and data structures, using tools like **ExifTool**, **Metadata Analyzer**, or **Autopsy** that parse metadata tags and extract detailed information about file origins and modifications.

Moreover, **Email Metadata Analysis** focuses on dissecting metadata associated with email communications, including sender and recipient addresses, message timestamps, subject lines, and attachment metadata, employing forensic software tools like **Encase Forensic**, **MailXaminer**, or **MessageExport** that analyze email headers, extract metadata attributes, and reconstruct email threads to establish communication patterns or timelines of events. Techniques such as `exiftool -a -u -g1 file.jpg` in ExifTool or `foremost -t jpeg -i image.dd` in Autopsy facilitate email metadata examination by extracting metadata from JPEG images or disk images for detailed forensic analysis.

Furthermore, **Document Metadata Forensics** encompasses the examination of metadata embedded within office documents such as Microsoft Word, Excel, or PDF files, focusing on attributes like document titles, author names, editing histories, and revision tracking information, utilizing forensic tools like **OLETools**, **PDF Stream Dumper**, or **Microsoft Office Metadata Cleaner (MOICE)** that parse document structures, extract metadata fields, and analyze document properties to determine document origins, editing activities, or version histories. Commands such as `pdf-parser --search "Title" file.pdf` in PDF Stream Dumper or `olebrowse.py file.doc` in OLETools enable document metadata forensics by examining document properties and extracting metadata attributes for thorough forensic scrutiny.

Additionally, **Image Metadata Interpretation** involves analyzing metadata embedded within digital images such as JPEG, PNG, or TIFF files, encompassing details like camera settings, GPS coordinates, timestamp information, and editing history, employing tools like **ExifTool**, **Forensic Image Analysis (FIA)**, or **PyExifTool** that parse image headers, extract EXIF metadata tags, and reconstruct image acquisition details or manipulation activities. Commands such as `exiftool -a -u -g1 image.jpg` in ExifTool or `forensic_image_analyzer.py -i image.jpg` in FIA facilitate image metadata interpretation by extracting camera settings, geolocation data, and timestamp information for comprehensive forensic analysis.

Moreover, **Network Packet Metadata Analysis** focuses on examining metadata embedded within network traffic packets, including source and destination IP addresses, port numbers, protocol types, packet timestamps, and session durations, using network forensic tools like **Wireshark**, **TCPDump**, or **NetworkMiner** that capture, analyze, and reconstruct network packet metadata to trace communication patterns, identify anomalies, or reconstruct digital evidence timelines. Techniques such as `tcpdump -i eth0 -w capture.pcap` in TCPDump or `tshark -r capture.pcap -T fields -e ip.src -e ip.dst` in Wireshark facilitate network packet metadata analysis by capturing packet headers, extracting metadata fields, and generating network traffic logs for forensic examination.

Furthermore, **Mobile Device Metadata Forensics** involves scrutinizing metadata embedded within mobile device artifacts such as call logs, SMS messages, GPS coordinates, and application usage histories, using mobile forensic tools like **Cellebrite UFED**, **XRY**, or **Oxygen Forensic Detective** that extract data from mobile device backups, analyze SQLite databases, and parse metadata attributes to reconstruct user activities or digital evidence timelines. Commands such as `ufed -e --package output.ufd -f device-backup.tar` in Cellebrite UFED or `oxygen -a -b backup-file.img` in Oxygen Forensic Detective enable mobile device metadata forensics by extracting call records, message timestamps, and application usage data for comprehensive forensic analysis.

Additionally, **Cloud Metadata Examination** involves analyzing metadata associated with cloud-based services such as Dropbox, Google Drive, or Microsoft OneDrive, including file access timestamps, user account details, sharing permissions, and IP addresses, using cloud forensic tools like **Magnet AXIOM Cloud**, **Cellebrite Cloud Analyzer**, or **F-Response Cloud Connector** that retrieve metadata from cloud storage APIs, analyze cloud activity logs, and reconstruct digital evidence timelines. Techniques such as `axiom-cloud -a -t token -i account-email` in Magnet AXIOM Cloud or `cloudanalyzer -u username -p password -d dropbox` in Cellebrite Cloud Analyzer facilitate cloud metadata examination by accessing file access logs, user session details, and sharing activities for forensic investigation and analysis.

In summary, interpretation of metadata in forensic analysis spans file metadata examination, email metadata analysis, document metadata forensics, image metadata interpretation, network packet metadata analysis, mobile device metadata forensics, and cloud metadata examination techniques that enable forensic investigators to extract, analyze, and reconstruct digital evidence from diverse sources. By leveraging these methods and tools, forensic analysts can uncover crucial details about digital artifacts, establish evidence timelines, and support investigative or legal proceedings by interpreting metadata attributes, ensuring data integrity, and enhancing the efficacy of digital forensic examinations in modern investigative landscapes.

Chapter 8: Introduction to Incident Reporting and Documentation

Interpretation of metadata in forensic analysis is a critical aspect of digital investigations, providing valuable insights into the origins, characteristics, and usage history of digital artifacts such as files, documents, emails, and multimedia content. Metadata, often described as "data about data," encompasses a range of attributes embedded within digital files or generated during digital interactions, offering forensic examiners a wealth of contextual information crucial for establishing timelines, verifying authenticity, and uncovering the circumstances surrounding digital activities. **File Metadata Analysis** is a foundational technique involving the examination of metadata attributes embedded within files, including creation dates, modification timestamps, file sizes, and author information, using forensic tools like **ExifTool**, **Metadata Analyzer**, or **Autopsy** that parse file headers and metadata tags to extract detailed information about file origins and editing history.

In digital investigations, **Email Metadata Examination** plays a pivotal role in reconstructing communication patterns and establishing timelines of email exchanges, scrutinizing metadata such as sender and recipient addresses, message timestamps, subject lines, and attachment details using forensic tools like **Encase Forensic**, **MailXaminer**, or **MessageExport** that parse email header information, extract metadata attributes, and reconstruct email threads to facilitate forensic analysis and evidentiary validation. Commands such as `exiftool -a -u -g1 file.jpg` in ExifTool or `foremost -t jpeg -i image.dd` in

Autopsy are instrumental in extracting metadata from JPEG images or disk images, enabling detailed scrutiny of email metadata to uncover communication histories and trace digital footprints crucial in forensic investigations.

Moreover, **Document Metadata Forensics** involves analyzing metadata embedded within office documents such as Microsoft Word, Excel, or PDF files, encompassing properties like document titles, author names, editing histories, and revision tracking information. Forensic software tools like **OLETools**, **PDF Stream Dumper**, or **Microsoft Office Metadata Cleaner (MOICE)** facilitate document metadata forensics by parsing document structures, extracting metadata fields, and analyzing document properties to ascertain document origins, editing activities, or version histories. Techniques such as `pdf-parser --search "Title" file.pdf` in PDF Stream Dumper or `olebrowse.py file.doc` in OLETools provide forensic analysts with the means to delve into document metadata, uncovering crucial details that support investigative findings and evidentiary requirements.

Additionally, **Image Metadata Interpretation** is indispensable for scrutinizing metadata embedded within digital images such as JPEG, PNG, or TIFF files, which encompass attributes like camera make and model, GPS coordinates, timestamp information, and editing history. Tools like **ExifTool**, **Forensic Image Analysis (FIA)**, or **PyExifTool** are employed to parse image headers, extract EXIF metadata tags, and reconstruct image acquisition details or manipulation activities. Commands such as `exiftool -a -u -g1 image.jpg` in ExifTool or `forensic_image_analyzer.py -i image.jpg` in FIA are pivotal in extracting camera settings, geolocation data, and timestamp information crucial for establishing the authenticity and provenance of digital images in forensic investigations.

Furthermore, **Network Packet Metadata Analysis** is essential for reconstructing network communication patterns, identifying suspicious activities, and tracing digital evidence timelines by examining metadata embedded within network traffic packets. Attributes such as source and destination IP addresses, port numbers, protocol types, packet timestamps, and session durations are analyzed using network forensic tools like **Wireshark**, **TCPDump**, or **NetworkMiner** that capture, analyze, and reconstruct network packet metadata. Techniques such as `tcpdump -i eth0 -w capture.pcap` in TCPDump or `tshark -r capture.pcap -T fields -e ip.src -e ip.dst` in Wireshark enable forensic analysts to capture packet headers, extract metadata fields, and generate network traffic logs crucial for detecting intrusions, analyzing network behavior, and reconstructing digital evidence chains in forensic investigations.

Moreover, **Mobile Device Metadata Forensics** involves extracting and analyzing metadata embedded within mobile device artifacts such as call logs, SMS messages, GPS coordinates, and application usage histories. Tools like **Cellebrite UFED**, **XRY**, or **Oxygen Forensic Detective** facilitate data extraction from mobile device backups, SQLite databases, and application logs to reconstruct user activities and digital evidence timelines. Commands such as `ufed -e --package output.ufd -f device-backup.tar` in Cellebrite UFED or `oxygen -a -b backup-file.img` in Oxygen Forensic Detective empower forensic examiners to retrieve call records, message timestamps, and location data crucial for investigating mobile device usage patterns and verifying digital evidence authenticity.

Additionally, **Cloud Metadata Examination** plays a vital role in forensic investigations by analyzing metadata associated with cloud-based services such as Dropbox, Google Drive, or Microsoft OneDrive. Metadata attributes including file access timestamps, user account details, sharing permissions, and IP addresses are extracted using tools like **Magnet AXIOM Cloud**, **Cellebrite Cloud Analyzer**, or **F-Response Cloud Connector** that interface with cloud storage APIs, analyze activity logs, and reconstruct digital evidence timelines. Techniques such as `axiom-cloud -a -t token -i account-email` in Magnet AXIOM Cloud or `cloudanalyzer -u username -p password -d dropbox` in Cellebrite Cloud Analyzer facilitate cloud metadata examination, enabling forensic investigators to trace file access events, user interactions, and collaboration activities crucial for establishing accountability and validating digital evidence in cloud-based forensic examinations.

In summary, interpretation of metadata in forensic analysis encompasses a wide array of techniques and tools tailored to extract, analyze, and interpret metadata attributes embedded within digital artifacts across various platforms and data sources. By leveraging these methodologies and forensic software tools, investigators can uncover crucial details, establish timelines, verify authenticity, and reconstruct digital activities essential for supporting investigative findings, ensuring evidentiary integrity, and facilitating informed decisions in legal proceedings and cybersecurity incident response efforts.

Chapter 9: Legal and Ethical Considerations in Cyber Investigations

Laws and regulations impacting cyber investigations play a pivotal role in shaping the legal framework and procedural guidelines that govern how digital evidence is collected, analyzed, and used in legal proceedings, highlighting the **General Data Protection Regulation (GDPR)** in Europe, which mandates data protection and privacy for all individuals within the European Union, including the handling of personal data and the rights of data subjects. Additionally, the **California Consumer Privacy Act (CCPA)** imposes strict regulations on the collection, use, and sale of personal information by businesses operating in California, requiring them to disclose data practices and provide consumers with the option to opt out of data sharing.

In the United States, the **Electronic Communications Privacy Act (ECPA)** governs the interception of electronic communications and access to stored communications, with provisions regulating the disclosure of electronic communications and the acquisition of electronic communications in transit, requiring compliance with legal requirements and procedures. Furthermore, the **Computer Fraud and Abuse Act (CFAA)** in the United States addresses unauthorized access to computer systems and networks, prohibiting activities such as hacking, unauthorized access, and data theft, with penalties including fines and imprisonment for violations of the law.

Moreover, **Data Protection Laws**, such as the **Health Insurance Portability and Accountability Act (HIPAA)** in the United States, establish standards for the protection of health information and require healthcare providers, insurers, and their business associates to ensure the confidentiality, integrity, and availability of protected health information, with penalties for violations of patient privacy and data security. Additionally, the **Gramm-Leach-Bliley Act (GLBA)** in the United States requires financial institutions to safeguard sensitive customer information and protect against unauthorized access or use of customer financial data, imposing regulations on data protection practices and security measures.

In Europe, the **Network and Information Security Directive (NIS Directive)** establishes cybersecurity requirements for operators of essential services and digital service providers, requiring them to implement risk management measures, report significant cybersecurity incidents to national authorities, and cooperate with other member states to ensure cybersecurity resilience and protect against cyber threats. Moreover, the **Payment Card Industry Data Security Standard (PCI DSS)** establishes security requirements for businesses that process credit card transactions, requiring compliance with data protection measures, encryption protocols, and security controls to protect cardholder data from unauthorized access or disclosure.

Additionally, **Law Enforcement Access and Legal Processes** involve procedures for law enforcement agencies to obtain digital evidence, including search warrants, subpoenas, and court orders, requiring compliance with legal standards and procedural safeguards to ensure the admissibility of digital evidence in criminal investigations and prosecutions. The **Foreign Intelligence Surveillance Act (FISA)** in the United States regulates electronic surveillance and intelligence gathering activities conducted by federal agencies, requiring judicial oversight and approval for the collection of foreign intelligence information and the monitoring of communications involving foreign powers or agents of foreign powers.

Furthermore, **Cross-Border Data Transfer Regulations** govern the international transfer of personal data and digital evidence between jurisdictions, addressing issues of jurisdictional authority, data sovereignty, and privacy protection, with frameworks such as the **EU-US Privacy Shield** facilitating the transfer of personal data between the European Union and the United States, ensuring compliance with data protection principles and legal requirements. Moreover, **Cybercrime Legislation** addresses offenses related to cyber threats, attacks, and malicious activities, with laws such as the **Cybersecurity Act of 2015** in the United States establishing penalties for cybercriminal offenses, including unauthorized access, data theft, and computer fraud.

In summary, laws and regulations impacting cyber investigations encompass a complex and evolving legal landscape that establishes standards for data protection, privacy rights, electronic communications, cybersecurity resilience, and law enforcement access to digital evidence, ensuring compliance with legal requirements, procedural safeguards, and ethical standards in the conduct of cyber investigations and digital forensic examinations. By understanding and adhering to these legal frameworks, stakeholders can navigate regulatory challenges, protect individual rights, and enhance the effectiveness of cyber investigations in addressing cyber threats, safeguarding digital infrastructure, and preserving the integrity of digital evidence in legal proceedingsEthics in handling digital evidence are foundational principles that guide the conduct of forensic investigators, ensuring integrity, fairness, and accountability in the collection, preservation, analysis, and presentation of digital evidence throughout investigative processes, emphasizing the **International Organization for Standardization (ISO) 27037**, which provides guidelines for digital evidence handling and specifies procedures for the identification, collection, preservation, and presentation of digital evidence, ensuring compliance with legal and regulatory requirements. Furthermore, the **Association of Chief

Police Officers (ACPO) Guidelines** in the United Kingdom outline best practices for digital evidence handling, including procedures for securing crime scenes, documenting evidence recovery processes, and maintaining chain of custody records to ensure the admissibility and reliability of digital evidence in court proceedings.

In the United States, the **National Institute of Standards and Technology (NIST) Special Publication 800-101** provides guidance on forensic evidence handling, emphasizing the importance of maintaining data integrity, documenting forensic processes, and ensuring transparency in investigative practices to uphold ethical standards and legal requirements. Additionally, the **American Bar Association (ABA) Model Rules of Professional Conduct** outline ethical obligations for attorneys and legal professionals in handling digital evidence, including duties to preserve, disclose, and authenticate electronic evidence in litigation, ensuring fairness, reliability, and admissibility in legal proceedings.

Moreover, **Digital Evidence Integrity** is paramount in forensic investigations, involving techniques such as **Hash Calculation** using tools like **md5sum**, **sha256sum**, or **Hashdeep** that compute cryptographic hash values for digital files or disk images, ensuring data integrity, and verifying file authenticity by comparing hash values before and after evidence acquisition processes. Commands such as `md5sum file.txt` in Linux or `CertUtil -hashfile file.txt MD5` in Windows facilitate hash calculation to generate MD5 checksums and SHA-256 hashes, ensuring data integrity throughout forensic examinations and verifying the accuracy of digital evidence presented in court.

Additionally, **Chain of Custody Documentation** is essential in maintaining the chronological record of custody, control, and transfer of digital evidence from its initial collection through analysis and presentation in legal proceedings, utilizing tools like **Evidence Management Systems (EMS)** or **Digital Forensic Case Management Software** that automate chain of custody documentation, track evidence movements, and generate audit trails to ensure accountability and transparency in forensic investigations. Techniques such as `chain_of_custody add evidence001.txt -u investigator001 -d "2024-06-22" -l "Evidence collected from crime scene"` in EMS facilitate digital evidence tracking, documenting custodial responsibilities, and preserving the integrity of chain of custody records essential for evidentiary admissibility.

Furthermore, **Conflict of Interest Avoidance** is crucial in forensic investigations, requiring forensic examiners to disclose any affiliations, relationships, or interests that may compromise their objectivity, impartiality, or integrity in handling digital evidence, adhering to ethical guidelines and professional standards to maintain credibility and trustworthiness in forensic examinations. Moreover, **Data Privacy and

Confidentiality** are fundamental ethical considerations in handling digital evidence, emphasizing the **General Data Protection Regulation (GDPR)** in Europe and the **Health Insurance Portability and Accountability Act (HIPAA)** in the United States, which mandate data protection, confidentiality, and privacy safeguards for personal and sensitive information during forensic investigations.

Moreover, **Expert Witness Testimony** requires forensic examiners to provide impartial, objective, and scientifically sound opinions based on verifiable data, using **Expert Witness Reports** or **Affidavits** to document findings, methodologies, and conclusions derived from forensic examinations, ensuring clarity, credibility, and reliability in court testimony. Techniques such as `forensic_report generate -e investigator@example.com -t "Expert Witness Report" -f "file_analysis_report.pdf"` in forensic report generation tools facilitate the creation of detailed reports, presenting forensic findings, and supporting expert witness testimony with comprehensive documentation and evidence validation.

Additionally, **Continuing Education and Professional Development** are essential for forensic investigators to stay abreast of technological advancements, emerging threats, and evolving legal frameworks impacting digital evidence handling, participating in **Digital Forensics Training Programs**, **Certifications**, or **Conferences** that provide opportunities for skill development, knowledge enhancement, and ethical awareness in forensic practices. Moreover, **Peer Review and Quality Assurance** mechanisms ensure accountability and reliability in forensic examinations, involving **Case Review Boards**, **Quality Control Audits**, or **Independent Validation and Verification (IV&V)** processes that assess forensic methodologies, validate findings, and uphold ethical standards in digital evidence handling.

In summary, ethics in handling digital evidence encompass principles of integrity, transparency, confidentiality, and impartiality that guide forensic investigators in conducting ethical and responsible forensic examinations, ensuring compliance with legal requirements, maintaining data integrity, and upholding professional standards in the collection, analysis, and presentation of digital evidence in investigative and legal contexts

Chapter 10: Building a Foundation for Cyber Incident Response

Developing a comprehensive incident response plan (IRP) is essential for organizations to effectively mitigate, detect, respond to, and recover from cybersecurity incidents, beginning with **Risk Assessment** to identify potential threats, vulnerabilities, and risks to organizational assets, using tools such as **Nmap** or **OpenVAS** to scan network devices and systems for known vulnerabilities and weaknesses, enabling organizations to prioritize risks and allocate resources effectively in their incident response planning process. Furthermore, **Incident Response Team Formation** involves assembling a multidisciplinary team comprising stakeholders from IT, legal, communications, and management departments to ensure diverse expertise and perspectives in responding to incidents, facilitating effective communication, decision-making, and coordination throughout the incident response lifecycle.

Moreover, **Incident Identification and Classification** requires organizations to establish **Monitoring and Detection Mechanisms** such as **Security Information and Event Management (SIEM)** tools or **Intrusion Detection Systems (IDS)** that monitor network traffic, system logs, and endpoint activities for suspicious behavior or indicators of compromise (IoCs), enabling organizations to identify and classify incidents based on severity, impact, and potential risks to business operations. Techniques such as `tail -f /var/log/syslog` in Linux or `Get-EventLog -LogName Security -Newest 100 | Where-Object {$_.EventID -eq "4625"}` in PowerShell facilitate real-time log monitoring and event detection, enhancing incident response capabilities and facilitating prompt incident containment and mitigation efforts.

Additionally, **Incident Response Procedures** outline predefined steps, tasks, and workflows for responding to specific types of incidents, establishing **Incident Response Playbooks** or **Runbooks** that document response procedures, escalation paths, and communication protocols to guide incident responders in executing timely and effective response actions. Techniques such as `grep "ERROR" application.log | tail -n 100` in Linux or `Select-String -Path application.log -Pattern "ERROR" -Context 0,100` in PowerShell enable log analysis and pattern matching to identify anomalies or indicators of potential incidents, facilitating proactive incident response and containment measures to minimize impact and restore normal business operations swiftly.

Moreover, **Incident Containment and Eradication** involves isolating affected systems, stopping malicious activities, and removing threats from the environment to prevent further damage or data exfiltration, utilizing tools such as **Netstat**, **Task Manager**, or **Process Explorer** to identify suspicious processes or network connections, facilitating containment actions such as `netstat -ano | findstr "ESTABLISHED"` in Command Prompt or `Get-NetTCPConnection -State Established` in PowerShell to identify active network connections and processes, enabling incident responders to terminate malicious activities and mitigate ongoing threats effectively.

Furthermore, **Forensic Analysis and Investigation** require organizations to conduct detailed examinations of compromised systems and digital artifacts to determine the root cause of incidents, using **Forensic Imaging Tools** such as **dd**, **FTK Imager**, or **Encase Forensic** to create forensic images of disk drives or storage media, preserving digital evidence and ensuring data integrity throughout the investigation process. Techniques such as `dd if=/dev/sda of=image.dd bs=1M` in Linux or `dcopy.exe C:\Forensic\Drive1 E:\Forensic\Drive1` in FTK Imager facilitate disk imaging and data preservation, enabling forensic analysts to recover deleted files, analyze system configurations, and reconstruct incident timelines to support incident response efforts and legal proceedings.

Moreover, **Communication and Reporting** are critical components of incident response planning, involving **Incident Notification** to stakeholders, regulatory authorities, and affected parties in compliance with **Incident Reporting Requirements** outlined in data protection laws or industry regulations, utilizing **Email Alerts**, **Notifications**, or **Incident Response Platforms** like **PagerDuty** or **ServiceNow** to disseminate incident notifications, updates, and status reports to key stakeholders and response team members. Techniques such as `mail -s "Incident Notification" admin@example.com < incident_report.txt` in Linux or `Send-MailMessage -To "admin@example.com" -Subject "Incident Notification" -Body (Get-Content incident_report.txt)` in PowerShell facilitate automated email notifications and communication channels, ensuring transparency, accountability, and timely dissemination of critical information during incident response activities.

Additionally, **Incident Recovery and Lessons Learned** involve restoring affected systems, data, and services to normal operations and conducting **Post-Incident Reviews** or **After-Action Reports** to evaluate incident response effectiveness, identify areas for improvement, and implement **Corrective Actions** or **Remediation Plans** to strengthen organizational resilience and enhance incident response capabilities. Techniques such as `rsync -avz --delete /backup/ /data/` in Linux or `robocopy /mir /e /copyall /r:3 /w:5 /log:C:\Logs\robocopy.log /tee C:\Logs\robocopy_output.log` in PowerShell facilitate data recovery and system restoration processes, enabling organizations to mitigate operational disruptions, minimize financial losses, and enhance incident preparedness for future cybersecurity incidents.

In summary, developing a comprehensive incident response plan involves proactive risk assessment, effective team formation, robust incident identification and classification, well-defined response procedures, efficient incident containment and eradication, thorough forensic analysis and investigation, clear communication and reporting, diligent incident recovery efforts, and continuous improvement through post-incident reviews and lessons learned, ensuring organizations can respond swiftly and effectively to cybersecurity incidents, mitigate potential risks, and safeguard critical assets and data from evolving cyber threatsImplementing incident response exercises is crucial for organizations to validate and enhance their incident response capabilities, beginning with **Tabletop Exercises** that simulate cybersecurity incidents and facilitate discussions among key stakeholders, using tools such as **MS Teams** or **Zoom** to conduct virtual tabletop exercises, enabling participants to discuss incident scenarios, assess response strategies, and identify gaps in incident response plans. Additionally, **Functional Exercises** simulate real-world incident scenarios involving specific teams or departments, using tools like **Simulated Attack Platforms** such as **Cobalt Strike** or **Atomic Red Team**, deploying red team techniques such as `sudo nmap -sS -sV -p- -T4 target_IP` to simulate network reconnaissance and identify potential vulnerabilities, allowing blue teams to detect, analyze, and respond to simulated attacks effectively.

Moreover, **Full-Scale Exercises** replicate comprehensive incident scenarios across entire organizations or critical infrastructure sectors, utilizing **Incident Response Simulation Tools** such as **Mimikatz** or **Metasploit** to simulate advanced persistent threats (APTs) or ransomware attacks, deploying attack techniques like `mimikatz.exe privilege::debug sekurlsa::logonpasswords exit` to extract credentials and simulate credential theft, enabling incident response teams to practice incident detection, containment, eradication, and recovery strategies in a controlled environment.

Furthermore, **Scenario Development** involves creating realistic incident scenarios based on current cyber threats, regulatory requirements, or industry-specific risks, using **Scenario Planning Templates** or **Incident Simulation Platforms** like **Cymulate** or **RangeForce**, configuring scenario parameters and attack vectors to simulate phishing attacks, malware infections, or data breaches, enabling organizations to evaluate incident response readiness and improve incident handling procedures. Techniques such as `cymulate simulate --attack phishing --target user@example.com` facilitate simulated phishing attacks to assess user awareness and response effectiveness, enhancing organizational resilience against social engineering threats.

Additionally, **Incident Response Playbooks** are essential tools that document step-by-step procedures, response workflows, and decision-making criteria for specific incident types, leveraging **Automated Playbook Execution** using **Security Orchestration, Automation, and Response (SOAR)** platforms like **Splunk Phantom** or **Demisto**, automating incident response tasks such as `!run playbook-incident-response.yml` to orchestrate response actions, automate data enrichment, and streamline incident resolution processes, enhancing efficiency and consistency in incident response operations.

Moreover, **Participant Training and Education** are critical components of incident response exercises, providing **Training Modules** or **Cybersecurity Awareness Programs** that educate employees, incident responders, and stakeholders on incident response best practices, using **Training Simulators** or **Interactive Learning Platforms** such as **SANS NetWars** or **Cyberbit Range**, deploying gamified exercises and hands-on labs to simulate cyber threats, reinforce incident response skills, and foster a culture of vigilance and resilience within organizations.

Furthermore, **Post-Exercise Evaluation** involves conducting **After-Action Reviews** or **Incident Response Assessments** to evaluate exercise performance, identify strengths, weaknesses, and areas for improvement in incident response capabilities, using **Evaluation Metrics** and **Key Performance

Indicators (KPIs)** to measure response times, decision-making effectiveness, and communication protocols during simulated incidents, facilitating continuous improvement and refinement of incident response plans and procedures.

Additionally, **Regulatory Compliance** and **Industry Standards** mandate regular incident response exercises and evaluations to ensure compliance with data protection laws, regulatory requirements, and industry best practices, using **Audit and Compliance Frameworks** such as **ISO/IEC 27001** or **NIST Cybersecurity Framework**, conducting tabletop exercises or penetration testing exercises to assess organizational readiness, validate incident response controls, and demonstrate compliance with legal and regulatory obligations.

In summary, implementing incident response exercises is essential for organizations to enhance incident response capabilities, validate response procedures, train personnel, and strengthen resilience against cyber threats, using tabletop, functional, and full-scale exercises, scenario development, automated playbook execution, participant training, post-exercise evaluation, and regulatory compliance frameworks to simulate, assess, and improve incident response readiness and effectiveness in safeguarding critical assets, data, and operations from evolving cyber threats

BOOK 2
INTERMEDIATE CYBER FORENSICS
TECHNIQUES AND TOOLS FOR SECURITY
INVESTIGATORS

ROB BOTWRIGHT

Chapter 1: Advanced Data Acquisition Methods

Live data acquisition techniques are essential in digital forensics for capturing volatile information from live systems and devices without altering the state of the data, beginning with **Memory Forensics**, which involves extracting and analyzing volatile memory contents using tools such as **Volatility Framework** or **Magnet RAM Capture**, executing commands like `volatility -f memory_dump.raw imageinfo` to determine memory dump profile information, identifying running processes, network connections, and loaded kernel modules, enabling forensic analysts to gather evidence of active threats or suspicious activities in real-time.

Additionally, **Network Packet Capture** allows forensic investigators to capture and analyze network traffic for evidence of malicious activities or unauthorized access attempts, utilizing **Wireshark** or **Tcpdump** tools to capture packets, filter traffic, and analyze packet contents, executing commands like `tcpdump -i eth0 -w capture.pcap` to capture network packets from Ethernet interface eth0 and store them in a pcap file for subsequent analysis using Wireshark's graphical interface or command-line tools.

Moreover, **Remote System Imaging** facilitates forensic data acquisition from remote systems over a network connection, using **DD** or **Netcat** (nc) commands to create disk images and transfer them securely between systems, executing commands like `nc -l -p 12345 > image.dd` on the remote system to listen on port 12345 and redirect the output to an image file, while on the local system, running `nc remote_host_ip 12345 < /dev/sda` to connect to the remote host and stream the disk image data to the local system.

Furthermore, **Live System Forensic Analysis** involves examining live systems and devices for evidence of active threats or unauthorized access using **Forensic Analysis Tools** such as **Autopsy**, **FTK Imager**, or **Sleuth Kit**, executing commands like `autopsy -l /dev/sda` to launch Autopsy GUI and analyze a live system's disk or `fls -r /dev/sdb1` in Sleuth Kit to list allocated and unallocated files from a specific partition, facilitating file system analysis, metadata examination, and artifact discovery in real-time.

Additionally, **Remote Memory Acquisition** enables forensic investigators to capture memory dumps from remote systems for offline analysis using **LiME** (Linux Memory Extractor) or **WinPmem** tools, executing commands like `lime-forensic -r -o memory_dump.lime` to create a memory dump file remotely, preserving volatile memory contents for subsequent forensic analysis and investigation using memory analysis frameworks like Volatility or Rekall.

Moreover, **Live Data Collection from Mobile Devices** involves acquiring volatile data from smartphones or tablets using **Mobile Forensic Tools** such as **Cellebrite UFED**, **XRY**, or **Oxygen Forensic Detective**, executing commands like `adb pull /data/data/com.example.app/databases/app.db` to pull SQLite database files from Android devices using Android Debug Bridge (ADB), enabling forensic examiners to extract application data, call logs, messages, and GPS coordinates from mobile devices for forensic analysis and evidentiary purposes.

Furthermore, **Live Data Collection from IoT Devices** is critical in IoT forensics for acquiring volatile data from connected devices and sensors using **IoT Forensic Tools** such as **IoT Inspector** or **Firmwalker**, executing commands like `firmwalker -d /dev/ttyUSB0` to analyze firmware images and extract file system contents from IoT devices via USB interface, facilitating forensic analysis of IoT device configurations, network communications, and sensor data for investigating cyber-physical attacks or unauthorized access attempts.

Additionally, **Live Data Acquisition Best Practices** emphasize **Minimizing System Impact** by using forensically sound methods and tools that do not alter or compromise live data integrity, **Documenting Acquisition Processes** to maintain chain of custody and ensure admissibility of evidence in legal proceedings, and **Preserving Evidence Integrity** through cryptographic hashes and digital signatures to verify data authenticity and integrity throughout the forensic acquisition and analysis lifecycle.

Moreover, **Legal and Ethical Considerations** in live data acquisition require compliance with data protection laws, privacy regulations, and organizational policies governing data collection, handling, and disclosure, ensuring **Informed Consent** and **Warrant Requirements** for accessing and acquiring live data from systems, devices, or networks during forensic investigations.

In summary, live data acquisition techniques are indispensable in digital forensics for capturing volatile information from live systems and devices using memory forensics, network packet capture, remote system imaging, live system forensic analysis, remote memory acquisition, mobile and IoT device data collection, adhering to best practices, legal considerations, and ethical guidelines to preserve evidence integrity and facilitate effective forensic investigations. Forensic imaging best practices are crucial in digital forensics for creating bit-by-bit copies of storage media, beginning with **Verification of Source Media** to ensure its integrity and authenticity before imaging using tools such as **dc3dd**, executing commands like `dc3dd if=/dev/sda of=image.dd hash=md5,sha256 log=image_log.txt` to image a disk (/dev/sda) while generating MD5 and SHA-256 hashes for verification, providing a reliable baseline for subsequent forensic analysis and investigation.

Furthermore, **Write Blocking** mechanisms prevent inadvertent alteration of source media during imaging processes, utilizing hardware write blockers or **Software Write Protection** utilities like **FTK Imager** or **dc3dd**, executing commands like `ftkimager --writeprotect /dev/sda` to enable write protection on a device (/dev/sda), ensuring forensic soundness and maintaining chain of custody throughout the imaging process.

Moreover, **Chain of Custody Documentation** is essential for documenting the handling, storage, and transfer of forensic images, utilizing **Hash Verification** to validate image integrity and authenticity using commands like `md5sum image.dd` or `sha256sum image.dd` to calculate MD5 or SHA-256 hashes of a forensic image (image.dd), ensuring data integrity and facilitating evidence admissibility in legal proceedings.

Additionally, **Data Verification** involves comparing hash values of the original source media with those of the forensic image to ensure data consistency and accuracy using tools like **HashCalc** or **md5deep**, executing commands like `hashdeep -a -k image_hashes.txt` to verify hash values against a predefined list (image_hashes.txt) and confirm the integrity of the forensic image, enabling forensic examiners to detect and mitigate data tampering or corruption effectively.

Furthermore, **Forensic Imaging Tools** such as **dd**, **dcfldd**, or **EnCase Forensic** facilitate disk imaging and verification processes, executing commands like `dd if=/dev/sdb of=image.img bs=1M` to image a disk (/dev/sdb) and specifying block size (bs=1M) for optimal performance, ensuring complete and accurate acquisition of digital evidence while adhering to forensic imaging best practices.

Moreover, **Image Format Selection** is critical for compatibility and data preservation, choosing **RAW (dd)**, **E01 (Encase)**, or **AFF (Advanced Forensic Format)** based on investigation requirements and forensic tool support, executing commands like `ewfacquire -t dd /dev/sdc image.e01` to acquire a disk (/dev/sdc) in Encase E01 format using **EWF Tools**, ensuring forensic image compatibility and metadata preservation for comprehensive analysis and interpretation.

Additionally, **Documentation and Metadata** include capturing pertinent information such as **Device Serial Numbers**, **Date and Time**, **Imaging Parameters**, and **Chain of Custody Logs**, utilizing tools like **Digital Evidence Bags (DEB)** or **Sleuth Kit** to annotate and document forensic imaging processes, maintaining data integrity and audit trails throughout forensic investigations.

Moreover, **Error Handling and Validation** involves implementing **Error Correction Mechanisms** during imaging processes, using tools like **ddrescue** or **R-Studio** to recover data from damaged or corrupted storage media, executing commands like `ddrescue -d -r 3 /dev/sdd image_rescue.dd logfile.txt` to rescue data from a faulty device (/dev/sdd) with retry limit (r=3) and log progress to a file (logfile.txt), ensuring comprehensive data recovery and forensic analysis capabilities.

Furthermore, **Compression and Encryption** of forensic images protect sensitive data and optimize storage resources using **gzip**, **7-Zip**, or **Veracrypt**, executing commands like `gzip image.dd` to compress a forensic image (image.dd) or `veracrypt -c /dev/sde` to encrypt a disk (/dev/sde) before imaging, ensuring data confidentiality and integrity during storage and transmission.

Moreover, **Secure Storage and Transmission** involve using **Cryptographic Hashes** and **Encryption Algorithms** to safeguard forensic images, storing them on **Encrypted Drives** or **Forensic Servers** with restricted access controls, using tools like **TrueCrypt** or **BitLocker**, executing commands like `truecrypt -t /dev/sdf1 /mnt/truecrypt` to mount an encrypted partition (/dev/sdf1) to a mount point (/mnt/truecrypt) for secure data storage and transmission.

Additionally, **Quality Assurance** involves validating forensic imaging processes through **Peer Review**, **Third-Party Audits**, or **Validation Tools** like **FTK Imager** or **EnCase**, executing commands like `ftkimager --verify image.dd` to verify the integrity and accuracy of a forensic image (image.dd), ensuring adherence to forensic imaging best practices and regulatory compliance requirements.

In summary, forensic imaging best practices encompass verifying source media, implementing write protection, maintaining chain of custody documentation, performing data verification, utilizing forensic imaging tools, selecting appropriate image formats, documenting metadata, handling errors, securing compression and encryption, ensuring secure storage and transmission, and conducting quality assurance to preserve data integrity, facilitate forensic analysis, and support legal investigations effectively.

Chapter 2: File System Forensics Analysis

Analysis of NTFS file systems in digital forensics involves examining the structure, metadata, and content of NTFS partitions to uncover evidence of user activities, beginning with **Metadata Analysis** using tools like **Sleuth Kit**, executing commands like `fls -r /dev/sda1` to list allocated and unallocated files from an NTFS partition (/dev/sda1), revealing file system metadata such as file names, timestamps, and permissions, enabling forensic examiners to reconstruct user actions and timelines accurately.

Moreover, **File Allocation Table (FAT) Analysis** provides insights into file allocation and storage patterns within NTFS volumes, using tools such as **ntfsinfo** or **DiskInternals NTFS Recovery**, executing commands like `ntfsinfo /dev/sdb1` to display NTFS volume information and examine file system attributes, including cluster sizes, MFT entry sizes, and file compression settings, facilitating forensic analysis and data recovery processes.

Additionally, **Journal Analysis** plays a crucial role in NTFS forensics by analyzing **$LogFile** entries to track file system changes and modifications over time, using tools such as **LogParser** or **Forensic Toolkit (FTK)**, executing commands like `logparser -i:EVT -o:DAT "SELECT * FROM $LogFile WHERE EventID=3"` to parse and analyze NTFS journal records for specific events (EventID=3), including file creations, deletions, or modifications, enabling forensic investigators to reconstruct file system activities and establish timelines of user actions.

Furthermore, **Master File Table (MFT) Examination** is essential in NTFS analysis for accessing file metadata and attributes stored in MFT entries, utilizing tools like **MFT Parser** or **Encase Forensic**, executing commands like `mftparser -f image.dd` to parse and extract MFT records from a forensic image (image.dd), revealing information such as file names, timestamps, file sizes, and data extents, facilitating forensic analysis and data recovery efforts.

Moreover, **Deleted File Recovery** involves recovering deleted files and directories from NTFS volumes using **File Carving Tools** such as **Scalpel**, **PhotoRec**, or **TestDisk**, executing commands like `photorec /dev/sdc` to scan a disk (/dev/sdc) for deleted files and extract recoverable data based on file signatures and metadata, enabling forensic examiners to retrieve evidence of deleted user activities or data remnants for investigative purposes.

Additionally, **Alternate Data Stream (ADS) Analysis** examines hidden data streams within NTFS files using tools like **ADS Spy** or **Bulk Extractor**, executing commands like `ads -s -r /mnt/ntfs_volume` to recursively search and extract alternate data streams from an NTFS volume mounted at /mnt/ntfs_volume, revealing hidden content, metadata, or executables associated with files, facilitating forensic analysis of malicious activities or unauthorized data storage.

Furthermore, **Timeline Analysis** integrates metadata, MFT records, and journal entries to reconstruct chronological events and user actions within NTFS file systems, using tools like **Plaso** or **Timeline Explorer**, executing commands like `log2timeline.py /mnt/ntfs_volume/timeline.plaso /mnt/ntfs_volume/$LogFile` to parse NTFS journal records and create a timeline (timeline.plaso) of file system activities, enabling forensic investigators to correlate events, identify anomalies, and establish timelines of digital evidence.

Moreover, **Keyword Search and Pattern Matching** techniques enable forensic examiners to locate specific files, documents, or artifacts within NTFS volumes using **grep**, **find**, or **EnCase Forensic**, executing commands like `grep -iR "confidential" /mnt/ntfs_volume` to search for the keyword "confidential" recursively within files on an NTFS volume mounted at /mnt/ntfs_volume, facilitating targeted searches and retrieval of relevant digital evidence for forensic analysis.

Additionally, **Forensic Reporting and Documentation** encompass documenting findings, methodologies, and analysis results using **Forensic Report Templates** or **Case Management Systems** such as **Autopsy** or **X-Ways Forensics**, ensuring comprehensive documentation of NTFS analysis processes, findings, and conclusions for evidentiary purposes and presenting forensic evidence in legal proceedings or investigative reports effectively.

Moreover, **Hash Calculation and Verification** are integral to NTFS forensic analysis for validating data integrity and authenticity using tools like **md5sum**, **sha256sum**, or **Hashdeep**, executing commands like `md5sum image.dd` to calculate MD5 hashes of a forensic image (image.dd) and verify file integrity against known hash values, ensuring forensic soundness and reliability of digital evidence throughout the analysis and investigation lifecycle.

In summary, NTFS file system analysis in digital forensics encompasses metadata analysis, file allocation table examination, journal analysis, MFT inspection, deleted file recovery, ADS analysis, timeline reconstruction, keyword search, forensic reporting, hash calculation, and verification techniques to uncover evidence, reconstruct events, and support investigative efforts effectively. File metadata examination techniques are essential in digital forensics for analyzing and interpreting metadata attributes associated with files, beginning with **Basic Metadata Analysis**, which involves examining fundamental file attributes such as **File Name**, **File Size**, **File Type**, and **Timestamps** using tools like **Sleuth Kit**, executing commands like `ffind -t d /dev/sda1` to search for all directory entries (-t d) within a file system (/dev/sda1), revealing metadata information including file names, sizes, and timestamps, enabling forensic examiners to identify and classify digital artifacts for further analysis. Furthermore, **Timestamp Analysis** plays a crucial role in forensic investigations by analyzing file timestamps such as **Creation Time**, **Modification Time**, and **Access Time** using tools like **Autopsy** or **ExifTool**, executing commands like `exiftool -time:all /path/to/file` to display all timestamp information associated with a file (/path/to/file), facilitating timeline analysis and reconstruction of file access, modification, and creation events during forensic examinations.

Moreover, **Extended File Attributes (EAs)** examination involves analyzing additional metadata attributes associated with files in **NTFS** or **ext4** file systems using tools like **Getfattr** or **EAs Viewer**, executing commands like `getfattr -d /path/to/file` to display all extended attributes (-d) associated with a file (/path/to/file), revealing metadata information such as file author, version, or application-specific data, facilitating detailed forensic analysis and evidence reconstruction.

Additionally, **File Signature Analysis** enables forensic examiners to identify file types and formats based on unique signatures or magic numbers using tools like **TrID** or **File** command, executing commands like `trid /path/to/file` to analyze and identify file types by examining byte patterns and signatures within a file (/path/to/file), assisting in categorizing digital artifacts and determining their relevance to forensic investigations.

Furthermore, **Embedded Metadata Extraction** involves extracting metadata embedded within files such as **EXIF** (Exchangeable Image File Format) data from digital images or **ID3** tags from audio files using tools like **ExifTool** or **FFmpeg**, executing commands like `exiftool -a -u -g1 /path/to/image.jpg` to extract all metadata tags (-a), including unknown (-u) and group by 1 (-g1) from an image file (/path/to/image.jpg), revealing information such as camera settings, geolocation, or timestamps associated with digital media files, supporting forensic analysis and authenticity verification.

Moreover, **Metadata Visualization** techniques utilize tools like **Metadata Forensics Framework (MFF)** or **Metaspike** to visualize and interpret metadata relationships and dependencies within files and across digital artifacts, enabling forensic examiners to identify patterns, anomalies, or associations that may indicate suspicious activities or data manipulation during investigations.

Additionally, **Metadata Cross-Referencing** involves correlating metadata attributes from multiple files or digital artifacts to establish connections, timelines, or dependencies using tools like **Autopsy** or **X-Ways

Forensics**, executing commands like `autopsy -o /path/to/case` to open a forensic case (-o) and cross-reference metadata attributes across files within a case directory (/path/to/case), facilitating comprehensive analysis and reconstruction of digital evidence in forensic examinations.

Furthermore, **Cloud Metadata Analysis** involves examining metadata associated with files stored in cloud services such as **Google Drive**, **Dropbox**, or **OneDrive** using **Cloud Forensic Tools** or **APIs**, executing commands like `gdrive info file_id` to retrieve metadata information for a file (file_id) stored in Google Drive, enabling forensic examiners to analyze access logs, sharing activities, and version histories associated with cloud-stored digital artifacts.

Moreover, **Metadata Forensic Artifacts** encompass analyzing metadata artifacts left behind by applications or operating systems during file operations or digital interactions using **Registry Analysis** or **Prefetch Analysis**, executing commands like `regripper -r SYSTEM -p ExplorerRecentDocs` to parse and extract recent documents (-p ExplorerRecentDocs) from Windows registry hive (SYSTEM), revealing metadata entries such as file paths, access times, and user interactions, supporting forensic investigations and evidence reconstruction.

Additionally, **Anti-Forensic Techniques Detection** involves identifying and mitigating attempts to alter or manipulate file metadata using **File Integrity Checking** tools like **Tripwire** or **Open Source Tripwire**, executing commands like `tripwire --check` to verify file integrity and detect unauthorized changes to file metadata or attributes, ensuring forensic soundness and data reliability throughout investigations.

Furthermore, **Metadata Reporting and Documentation** involve documenting findings, methodologies, and analysis results using **Forensic Report Templates** or **Case Management Systems** such as **Cellebrite UFED** or **XRY**, ensuring comprehensive documentation of metadata examination techniques, findings, and conclusions for evidentiary purposes and presenting forensic evidence effectively in legal proceedings or investigative reports.

In summary, file metadata examination techniques encompass basic metadata analysis, timestamp analysis, extended file attributes examination, file signature analysis, embedded metadata extraction, metadata visualization, cross-referencing, cloud metadata analysis, forensic artifacts analysis, anti-forensic techniques detection, metadata reporting, and documentation techniques to uncover, analyze, and interpret metadata attributes associated with digital artifacts effectively in forensic investigations.

Chapter 3: Memory Forensics Techniques

The Volatility Framework is a powerful tool widely used in digital forensics and incident response for analyzing memory dumps and extracting valuable information from volatile memory images of Windows, Linux, macOS, and Android systems, starting with **Memory Dump Analysis**, where forensic investigators use commands like `volatility -f memdump.raw imageinfo` to identify the profile of a memory dump file (memdump.raw) and gather basic system information such as the operating system version, architecture, and build, providing crucial insights into the memory image's origin and context for subsequent analysis.

Process Analysis within the Volatility Framework involves examining running processes and their associated details, using commands like `volatility -f memdump.raw pslist` to list all running processes in a memory dump file (memdump.raw), displaying process identifiers (PIDs), parent process identifiers (PPIDs), process names, and creation times, enabling forensic examiners to identify suspicious or malicious processes and investigate their activities further.

Moreover, **Network Connection Analysis** using Volatility enables investigators to analyze network connections established during the memory capture, employing commands like `volatility -f memdump.raw connections` to enumerate active network connections in a memory dump file (memdump.raw), displaying source and destination IP addresses, port numbers, protocols, and connection states, facilitating the identification of network-based attacks or unauthorized communications within the compromised system.

Additionally, **File Extraction and Analysis** involves extracting files from memory dumps using Volatility plugins such as `dumpfiles`, executing commands like `volatility -f memdump.raw --profile=Win7SP1x64 dumpfiles -Q 0xADDRESS -D output_directory/` to extract files associated with a specific address (0xADDRESS) from a Windows 7 SP1 x64 memory dump (memdump.raw) into an output directory (output_directory/), enabling forensic examiners to recover and analyze suspicious files or artifacts present in volatile memory.

Furthermore, **Registry Hive Analysis** within Volatility enables forensic investigators to parse and examine Windows registry hives from memory dumps using plugins like `hivelist` and `printkey`, executing commands like `volatility -f memdump.raw hivelist` to list active registry hives in a memory dump file (memdump.raw) and identify their virtual addresses, followed by `volatility -f memdump.raw --profile=Win7SP1x64 printkey -o 0xADDRESS -K 'Software\Microsoft\Windows\CurrentVersion\Run'` to extract and display registry key values associated with the 'Run' key path in a Windows 7 SP1 x64 memory dump (memdump.raw), aiding in the identification of persistence mechanisms or malware configurations stored in the registry.

Moreover, **DLLs and Handles Analysis** involves examining loaded DLLs and open handles within memory dumps using Volatility plugins like `dlllist` and `handles`, executing commands like `volatility -f memdump.raw --profile=Win10x64 dlllist` to list loaded DLLs in a Windows 10 x64 memory dump (memdump.raw), revealing module base addresses, paths, and associated processes, followed by `volatility -f memdump.raw handles -p PID` to list handles owned by a specific process (PID) in a memory dump file (memdump.raw), facilitating forensic analysis of loaded modules and resource access within the volatile memory image.

Additionally, **Kernel Object Analysis** enables forensic examiners to investigate kernel objects and their properties using Volatility plugins such as `kdbgscan` and `kpcrscan`, executing commands like `volatility -f memdump.raw kdbgscan` to locate and analyze the Kernel Debugger Block (KDBG) structure in a memory dump file (memdump.raw), providing kernel version information and facilitating subsequent kernel object scans using `volatility -f memdump.raw --profile=Win10x64 kpcrscan` to scan and list Process Control Regions (PCR) associated with running processes in a Windows 10 x64 memory dump, assisting in identifying rootkit infections or stealthy kernel-level modifications.

Furthermore, **Timeline Reconstruction** within Volatility involves correlating timestamps and events extracted from memory dumps to reconstruct chronological sequences of activities using plugins like `timeliner` and `mactime`, executing commands like `volatility -f memdump.raw timeliner --output=body --output-file=timeline.csv` to generate a timeline (timeline.csv) of system events and artifacts extracted from a memory dump file (memdump.raw), facilitating timeline analysis and visualization of user actions, file creations, network connections, and other notable activities within the volatile memory image.

Moreover, **Anti-Forensic Techniques Detection** involves using Volatility to detect and analyze attempts to manipulate or obfuscate memory artifacts, employing techniques such as **Memory Integrity Checks** with plugins like `malfind` and `ldrmodules`, executing commands like `volatility -f memdump.raw malfind` to scan a memory dump file (memdump.raw) for suspicious processes and memory sections indicating potential malware presence or memory injection techniques, assisting in identifying and mitigating anti-forensic measures aimed at evading detection or analysis.

Additionally, **Memory Profile Creation** within Volatility involves creating custom memory profiles using the `vol.py --info` command to identify available profiles, followed by using the `vol.py --info | grep -i windows` command. Memory dump analysis methods are crucial in digital forensics and incident response, offering investigators deep insights into the volatile state of a computer system at a specific moment, facilitating thorough examination of **Memory Dump Acquisition**, where tools like `Magnet RAM Capture` or `FTK Imager` are employed to capture live memory dumps, executed via commands such as `magnet_ram_capture.exe --live`, ensuring real-time preservation of volatile memory contents for forensic analysis.

Memory Dump Format Identification is fundamental, with dumps typically in formats like **raw**, **hpa**, or **LiME**, determined using commands such as `file memdump.raw` to ascertain the format of a memory dump file, ensuring compatibility with forensic tools for subsequent analysis and investigation of digital evidence.

Memory Dump File Carving techniques involve extracting specific artifacts or data structures from memory dumps, facilitated by tools like `Volatility`, where commands like `volatility -f memdump.raw --profile=Win10x64 filescan` are used to scan for file system metadata and recover deleted or hidden files, aiding in the reconstruction of file system activities and retrieval of crucial evidence.

Memory Dump Parsing allows investigators to extract relevant information from memory dumps using plugins like `imageinfo` and `pslist`, with commands such as `volatility -f memdump.raw imageinfo` providing system details like OS version and architecture, essential for targeted analysis of memory artifacts.

Process Analysis within memory dump analysis involves examining running processes and their attributes, achieved through tools like `Volatility` with commands like `volatility -f memdump.raw pslist` to list active processes, displaying PIDs, PPIDs, and creation times, aiding in the identification and analysis of malicious processes or unauthorized activities.

Network Connection Analysis in memory dump analysis enables the examination of network connections established during the memory capture, using tools like `Volatility` with commands like `volatility -f memdump.raw connections` to enumerate active connections, detailing IPs, ports, protocols, and connection states, crucial for identifying potential network-based attacks or suspicious communications.

Registry Hive Analysis techniques involve parsing Windows registry hives from memory dumps using `Volatility`, where commands such as `volatility -f memdump.raw hivelist` list active hives and `volatility -f memdump.raw --profile=Win10x64 printkey -o 0xADDRESS -K 'Software\Microsoft\Windows\CurrentVersion\Run'` extract registry key values, aiding in identifying malware persistence mechanisms or configurations stored in the registry.

File Extraction and Analysis techniques within memory dump analysis involve extracting files from dumps using `Volatility` with plugins like `dumpfiles`, executed via commands like `volatility -f memdump.raw --profile=Win7SP1x64 dumpfiles -Q 0xADDRESS -D output_directory/`, facilitating recovery and analysis of suspicious files or artifacts from volatile memory.

Anti-Forensic Techniques Detection encompasses identifying attempts to manipulate or conceal memory artifacts, using tools like `Volatility` with plugins such as `malfind` and `ldrmodules`, with commands like `volatility -f memdump.raw malfind` scanning for suspicious processes or memory sections indicative of malware presence or injection techniques.

Memory Profile Creation involves creating custom profiles for specific memory dumps using commands like `vol.py --info` to list available profiles and `vol.py --info | grep -i windows` to filter profiles for Windows systems, ensuring accurate and effective forensic analysis and artifact extraction.

In summary, memory dump analysis methods encompass acquisition, format identification, file carving, parsing, process analysis, network connection analysis, registry hive analysis, file extraction and analysis, anti-forensic techniques detection, memory profile creation, and advanced techniques essential for uncovering evidence and insights vital to forensic investigations and incident response efforts. These methods form the backbone of digital forensic practices, providing comprehensive tools and techniques to analyze volatile memory contents and reconstruct system activities for investigative purposes.

Chapter 4: Network Forensics and Analysis

Packet capture and analysis are integral components of network forensics and cybersecurity operations, involving the **Deployment of Wireshark**, a widely used tool for capturing and analyzing network packets, initiated by launching Wireshark through the command `wireshark` in the terminal, enabling real-time monitoring and capturing of network traffic for forensic examination.

Packet Capture Techniques include using `tcpdump`, a command-line packet analyzer, with commands like `tcpdump -i eth0 -w capture.pcap` capturing packets from interface `eth0` and writing them to a file `capture.pcap`, facilitating the collection of network data for subsequent analysis and investigation.

Traffic Filtering and Analysis in packet capture involves filtering captured packets based on specific criteria using Wireshark's display filters, such as `tcp.port == 80` to filter packets on TCP port 80 (HTTP), allowing forensic analysts to focus on relevant network activities and identify potential security incidents or anomalies.

Protocol Analysis within packet capture examines the behavior and communication patterns of network protocols, with tools like Wireshark offering dissectors and decoders for protocols like **HTTP**, **DNS**, **FTP**, and **SMTP**, enabling detailed inspection of protocol headers, payloads, and interactions for forensic examination.

Session Reconstruction techniques involve reconstructing network sessions and conversations from captured packets using tools like Wireshark, leveraging features such as `Follow TCP Stream` to reconstruct and analyze the entire TCP session contents, aiding in understanding communication flows and identifying suspicious activities or data exfiltration.

Traffic Pattern Analysis in packet capture identifies patterns and trends in network traffic using statistical tools and techniques, with commands like `tshark -r capture.pcap -qz io,stat,60,"SUM(frame.len)frame.len"`, generating traffic statistics from a pcap file `capture.pcap`, helping analysts detect anomalies or deviations from normal network behavior.

Malware Traffic Analysis involves analyzing network traffic associated with malware infections using packet capture tools like Wireshark, where analysts can filter packets by `ip.src == malicious_IP` to identify traffic originating from a known malicious IP address, assisting in malware identification, behavior analysis, and containment efforts.

Incident Response Packet Capture techniques focus on capturing network packets during incident response activities, with commands like `tcpdump -i eth0 -w incident_capture.pcap host victim_IP`, capturing packets exchanged between the victim and a specific IP address (`victim_IP`) for forensic analysis and investigation of security incidents.

Forensic Artifact Extraction from packet captures includes extracting files or artifacts transferred over the network, using Wireshark's `File > Export Objects > HTTP` feature to export HTTP objects like images, documents, or executables from captured packets, aiding in the reconstruction of digital evidence and forensic analysis.

Network Traffic Visualization techniques involve visualizing captured network traffic using tools like `Wireshark` or `tcptrace`, where analysts can use `tcptrace -r capture.pcap` to generate visual graphs and charts depicting network communication patterns, facilitating a clearer understanding of network behaviors and interactions.

Encrypted Traffic Analysis addresses the challenge of analyzing encrypted network traffic, with tools like Wireshark capable of decrypting SSL/TLS traffic using pre-shared keys (`SSLKEYLOGFILE`), enabling forensic examination and analysis of encrypted communications for incident response and cybersecurity investigations.

In summary, packet capture and analysis are essential in network forensics and cybersecurity operations, encompassing techniques for deployment, traffic filtering, protocol analysis, session reconstruction, traffic pattern analysis, malware traffic analysis, incident response, forensic artifact extraction, network traffic visualization, and encrypted traffic analysis. These methods provide critical capabilities for monitoring, analyzing, and investigating network activities, enabling cybersecurity professionals and forensic analysts to detect, mitigate, and respond to security incidents effectively. Intrusion Detection System (IDS) logs analysis is a critical aspect of cybersecurity operations, involving the examination and interpretation of **IDS Log Collection**, where logs from IDS sensors such as Snort or Suricata are collected and stored using commands like `tcpdump -i eth0 -w ids_capture.pcap host IDS_IP`, capturing network packets related to IDS alerts for further analysis and investigation.

Log Parsing and Normalization techniques include parsing IDS logs to extract relevant fields and normalize data formats using tools like `grep` or `awk`, with commands such as `grep "Alert" ids.log` filtering IDS logs for alerts or `awk -F',' '{print $3, $4, $5}' ids.log` to extract and display specific fields (e.g., timestamp, source IP, destination IP) from IDS logs, facilitating structured data analysis and correlation.

Alert Correlation involves correlating IDS alerts with logs from other security devices or systems using tools like `Elasticsearch` and `Kibana`, where commands like `curl -X GET "http://localhost:9200/_search?q=IDS_alert"` query Elasticsearch for IDS alerts stored in an index, enabling analysts to correlate events and identify patterns indicating potential security incidents.

Signature Analysis examines IDS alerts based on predefined signatures or rules using tools like `Snort`, where rules are analyzed and managed using commands like `snort -c /etc/snort/snort.conf -l /var/log/snort/ -A console` to start Snort with a specified configuration file (`snort.conf`), monitoring network traffic and generating alerts based on signature matches, aiding in the identification of known attack patterns or malicious activities.

Behavioral Analysis in IDS logs involves analyzing network behavior patterns and anomalies using statistical methods and machine learning algorithms, with tools like `Splunk` or `ELK stack`, where commands like `splunk search "sourcetype=snort"` query Splunk for IDS logs indexed as `snort`, enabling analysts to detect abnormal behaviors indicative of potential security breaches or insider threats.

Incident Response based on IDS logs includes responding to alerts and incidents identified through IDS analysis, with commands like `suricata-update` updating Suricata rulesets for enhanced threat detection and `suricata -c /etc/suricata/suricata.yaml -i eth0` starting Suricata with a specified configuration file (`suricata.yaml`) on interface `eth0` to monitor and analyze network traffic in real-time.

Forensic Investigation techniques leverage IDS logs for forensic analysis and reconstruction of security incidents, using commands like `grep "Unauthorized Access" ids.log` to search IDS logs for unauthorized access attempts or `tshark -r ids_capture.pcap -Y "alert.signature == 'ET INFO Suspicious activity detected'"` to filter IDS alerts from a packet capture file (`ids_capture.pcap`) based on a specific signature, aiding in the identification and attribution of security events.

Anomaly Detection in IDS logs involves detecting unusual or unexpected patterns in network traffic using anomaly detection algorithms or heuristics, with commands like `zeekctl deploy` deploying Zeek sensors for network traffic monitoring and anomaly detection, enabling proactive identification of abnormal behaviors indicative of potential security threats.

Threat Intelligence Integration incorporates threat intelligence feeds into IDS logs analysis using tools like `Suricata` or `Snort`, where commands like `suricata -c /etc/suricata/suricata.yaml -i eth0 --set "default-rule-path=/etc/suricata/rules"` start Suricata with custom rule paths (`/etc/suricata/rules`) for enhanced threat detection based on up-to-date threat intelligence data, enabling proactive defense against emerging threats.

Visualization and Reporting techniques involve visualizing IDS alerts and events using tools like `Grafana` or `Kibana`, where commands like `kibana` start Kibana for visualizing IDS log data stored in Elasticsearch indices, facilitating the creation of dashboards and reports to communicate security incidents and trends effectively.

In summary, IDS logs analysis encompasses log collection, parsing, normalization, alert correlation, signature analysis, behavioral analysis, incident response, forensic investigation, anomaly detection, threat intelligence integration, visualization, and reporting. These techniques are essential for monitoring, analyzing, and responding to security threats effectively, enabling organizations to protect their networks and data from cyber threats and attacks.

Chapter 5: Mobile Device Forensics

iOS device forensics is a specialized field within digital forensics that focuses on extracting and analyzing data from Apple's iOS devices, encompassing **Physical Acquisition Techniques**, where devices are imaged using tools like `GrayKey` or `Cellebrite UFED`, initiated by connecting the device and launching the tool to perform a physical extraction of the device's storage, capturing a bit-by-bit image for forensic analysis.

Logical Acquisition Methods involve extracting data from iOS devices through software-based methods like `iTunes Backup`, where commands like `idevicebackup2 backup --full /path/to/backup` create a full backup of the device's data, including contacts, messages, and app data, stored in an encrypted format for subsequent forensic examination.

File System Analysis includes examining the file system of iOS devices using tools like `XRY` or `Oxygen Forensic Detective`, where commands like `xry -i image.dd` analyze a forensic image (`image.dd`) of the device, enabling forensic analysts to recover deleted files, analyze file metadata, and reconstruct user activities for investigative purposes.

Data Parsing and Decoding techniques involve parsing and decoding iOS data formats such as `SQLite Databases`, where commands like `sqlite3 sms.db "SELECT * FROM messages;"` query the SQLite database (`sms.db`) containing SMS messages, extracting information like timestamps, sender, and message content for forensic analysis.

Timeline Analysis in iOS device forensics includes creating timelines of user activities and events using tools like `Autopsy` or `Sleuth Kit`, where commands like `log2timeline /path/to/image.dd` create a timeline (`timeline.csv`) from a forensic image (`image.dd`), documenting file accesses, app usage, and system events for chronological analysis.

App Data Extraction techniques involve extracting data stored within iOS applications using tools like `Mobiledit Forensic Express`, where commands like `mobiledit_forensic -i backup.ab -a --appdata` extract app data (`backup.ab`) from an iOS backup file, facilitating the recovery of application-specific information crucial for forensic investigations.

Cloud Data Analysis encompasses analyzing data synced with iCloud using tools like `Elcomsoft Phone Breaker`, where commands like `epb_cloud -u username -p password -s icloud` authenticate and download iCloud backups (`icloud`) containing synced data such as photos, contacts, and documents, aiding in comprehensive forensic analysis.

Location Data Examination involves analyzing GPS and Wi-Fi location data stored on iOS devices using tools like `iBackupBot`, where commands like `ibackupbot -d "LocationDomain"` extract location data from an iOS backup (`backup.ibackup`), mapping device movements and locations based on stored coordinates and timestamps.

Messaging and Social Media Analysis in iOS forensics includes extracting and analyzing messages and social media communications using tools like `Celebrite Physical Analyzer`, where commands like `celebrite_analyzer -i backup.cba -a --messages` parse and analyze messages (`backup.cba`) from popular messaging apps like WhatsApp and Facebook Messenger, uncovering communication details and attachments.

Metadata Interpretation techniques involve interpreting metadata from iOS device artifacts such as photos and documents using tools like `ExifTool`, where commands like `exiftool image.jpg` extract and display metadata (`image.jpg`) like camera settings, timestamps, and GPS coordinates, providing context for forensic analysis and investigation.

Password and Encryption Analysis includes analyzing password-protected files and encrypted data on iOS devices using tools like `Passware Kit Forensic`, where commands like `passware -p encrypted_file.pfx --passwords=passwords.txt` attempt to decrypt (`encrypted_file.pfx`) using a list of passwords (`passwords.txt`), enabling access to encrypted content for forensic examination.

Forensic Reporting involves creating detailed reports and documentation from iOS forensic analysis using tools like `X-Ways Forensics`, where commands like `xways -r report.txt` generate a comprehensive forensic report (`report.txt`) detailing findings, analysis methods, and conclusions for legal or investigative purposes.

In summary, iOS device forensics encompasses physical and logical acquisition techniques, file system analysis, data parsing and decoding, timeline analysis, app data extraction, cloud data analysis, location data examination, messaging and social media analysis, metadata interpretation, password and encryption analysis, and forensic reporting. These techniques are essential for forensic investigators and law enforcement agencies to extract, analyze, and interpret digital evidence from iOS devices, supporting criminal investigations, legal proceedings, and incident response efforts effectively. Android device forensics is a specialized area within digital forensics that involves extracting and analyzing data from Android-based smartphones and tablets, encompassing **Physical Acquisition Techniques** such as `ADB` (Android Debug Bridge) commands like `adb pull /data/data/com.example.app/databases/database.db /path/to/local/directory` for pulling SQLite database files (`database.db`) from Android devices to a local directory, enabling forensic analysis of app data and user activities.

Logical Acquisition Methods involve extracting data from Android devices through `ADB backup` commands like `adb backup -f backup.ab -apk com.example.app`, creating a full backup (`backup.ab`) including APK files (`-apk`) of the specified app (`com.example.app`), stored in an encrypted format for subsequent forensic examination.

File System Analysis includes examining the file system of Android devices using tools like `Autopsy` or `Encase`, where commands like `adb shell ls -l /sdcard/` list files (`ls -l`) on the device's SD card (`/sdcard/`), aiding in the recovery of deleted files, analyzing file metadata, and reconstructing user activities for forensic investigation.

Data Parsing and Decoding techniques involve parsing and decoding Android data formats such as `SQLite Databases`, where commands like `sqlite3 /data/data/com.example.app/databases/database.db "SELECT * FROM messages;"` query the SQLite database (`database.db`) for messages (`SELECT * FROM messages;`), extracting information like timestamps, sender, and message content crucial for forensic analysis.

Timeline Analysis in Android device forensics includes creating timelines of user activities and events using tools like `Sleuth Kit`, where commands like `mactime -d -z GMT /path/to/image.dd` create a timeline (`mactime`) from a forensic image (`image.dd`), documenting file accesses, app usage, and system events for chronological analysis.

App Data Extraction techniques involve extracting data stored within Android applications using tools like `AFLogical`, where commands like `aflogical -b backup.ab -a com.example.app` extract app data (`-a com.example.app`) from an Android backup (`backup.ab`), facilitating the recovery of application-specific information crucial for forensic investigations.

Cloud Data Analysis encompasses analyzing data synced with Google services using tools like `Google Takeout`, where commands like `google_takeout -u username@gmail.com -p password -s drive` authenticate and download Google Drive data (`drive`) synced with an Android device, aiding in comprehensive forensic analysis of cloud-stored information.

Location Data Examination involves analyzing GPS and Wi-Fi location data stored on Android devices using tools like `Android Location History`, where commands like `adb shell dumpsys location` query the device's location service (`dumpsys location`), mapping device movements and locations based on stored coordinates and timestamps for forensic investigation.

Messaging and Social Media Analysis in Android forensics includes extracting and analyzing messages and social media communications using tools like `MobiKin Doctor for Android`, where commands like `mobikin -i backup.ab -m --messages` parse and analyze messages (`-m`) from an Android backup (`backup.ab`), uncovering communication details and attachments crucial for forensic examinations.

Metadata Interpretation techniques involve interpreting metadata from Android device artifacts such as photos and documents using tools like `ExifTool`, where commands like `exiftool image.jpg` extract and display metadata (`image.jpg`) such as camera settings, timestamps, and GPS coordinates, providing context for forensic analysis and investigation.

Password and Encryption Analysis includes analyzing password-protected files and encrypted data on Android devices using tools like `John the Ripper`, where commands like `john -format=zip2 hashfile.txt` attempt to crack (`-format=zip2`) password hashes (`hashfile.txt`) for encrypted ZIP files, enabling access to encrypted content crucial for forensic examination.

Forensic Reporting involves creating detailed reports and documentation from Android forensic analysis using tools like `Cellebrite UFED Physical Analyzer`, where commands like `cellebrite -r report.pdf` generate a comprehensive forensic report (`report.pdf`) detailing findings, analysis methods, and conclusions for legal or investigative purposes.

In summary, Android device forensics encompasses physical and logical acquisition techniques, file system analysis, data parsing and decoding, timeline analysis, app data extraction, cloud data analysis, location data examination, messaging and social media analysis, metadata interpretation, password and encryption analysis, and forensic reporting. These techniques are essential for forensic investigators and law enforcement agencies to extract, analyze, and interpret digital evidence from Android devices, supporting criminal investigations, legal proceedings, and incident response efforts effectively.

Chapter 6: Malware Analysis and Reverse Engineering

Static and dynamic malware analysis techniques are fundamental processes in cybersecurity aimed at understanding the behavior, functionality, and impact of malicious software on systems and networks. **Static Analysis** involves examining malware without executing it, relying on methods such as `hashing`, where commands like `md5sum malware.exe` generate a hash (`md5sum`) value of a malware executable (`malware.exe`), allowing analysts to compare it against known malware hashes to identify previously identified threats.

Code Decompilation techniques, like `IDA Pro`, involve commands that open malware executables (`malware.exe`) for disassembly and analysis, enabling analysts to examine the assembly code, identify functions, and understand the logic behind the malware's operations.

String Extraction involves using tools like `strings`, where commands like `strings malware.exe` extract readable strings from a malware executable (`malware.exe`), revealing clues about hardcoded URLs, registry keys, or command-and-control (C2) server addresses embedded within the malware code.

Metadata Examination techniques include analyzing metadata of malware files using tools like

`ExifTool`, where commands like `exiftool malware.exe` extract metadata (`malware.exe`) such as file creation date, author information, or compiler details, providing insights into the malware's origin and development environment.

Packing and Obfuscation analysis involves unpacking and deobfuscating malware binaries using tools like `PEiD` or `UPX`, where commands like `upx -d malware_packed.exe` unpack (`-d`) a UPX-packed (`upx`) malware executable (`malware_packed.exe`), revealing the original code for further static analysis.

Behavioral Analysis techniques focus on observing malware's actions in a controlled environment, such as `sandboxing` using tools like `Cuckoo Sandbox`, where commands like `cuckoo submit malware_sample.exe` submit (`submit`) a malware sample (`malware_sample.exe`) to a sandbox environment (`cuckoo`), monitoring its behavior, network communications, and system impact.

Dynamic Code Analysis involves running malware in a controlled environment using tools like `Procmon` (Process Monitor), where commands like `procmon.exe /Minimized /Backingfile log.pml` monitor (`/Backingfile log.pml`) malware execution (`procmon.exe`), capturing system calls, file accesses, and registry modifications for behavioral analysis.

Memory Analysis techniques examine malware artifacts in system memory using tools like `Volatility`, where commands like `volatility -f memory_dump.raw imageinfo` analyze (`-f memory_dump.raw`) a memory dump (`imageinfo`), identifying running processes, network connections, and injected code associated with malware activity.

Network Traffic Analysis involves capturing and analyzing malware's network communications using tools like `Wireshark`, where commands like `wireshark -i eth0` capture (`-i eth0`) and analyze live network traffic (`wireshark`), revealing communication protocols, data payloads, and command-and-control server interactions.

Reverse Engineering techniques involve disassembling and analyzing malware code using tools like `Ghidra`, where commands like `ghidraRun` open (`ghidraRun`) a malware executable (`malware.exe`), enabling analysts to decompile and understand the malware's logic, identifying vulnerabilities or backdoor mechanisms.

Automated Analysis techniques include leveraging automated malware analysis platforms like `VirusTotal`, where commands like `virustotal-cli -f malware_sample.exe` submit (`-f malware_sample.exe`) a malware sample (`virustotal-cli`) for analysis, obtaining multiple antivirus scan results and behavioral reports.

Heuristic Analysis involves applying heuristic rules and pattern recognition to identify potentially malicious behavior or characteristics in malware samples, aiding in detection and classification using tools integrated with security solutions like `YARA`, where commands like `yara -r rules.yar malware_samples/` apply (`-r rules.yar`) YARA rules (`rules.yar`) to scan malware samples (`malware_samples/`), detecting specific patterns indicative of malicious activity.

Report Generation encompasses creating detailed reports and documentation from malware analysis using tools like `REMnux`, where commands like `malware-analysis-report -r analysis_report.pdf` generate (`-r analysis_report.pdf`) a comprehensive malware analysis report (`malware-analysis-report`), documenting findings, methodologies, and recommendations for incident response or mitigation strategies.

In summary, static and dynamic malware analysis techniques encompass a range of methodologies and tools crucial for cybersecurity professionals to analyze and understand the behavior, functionality, and impact of malicious software. These techniques enable effective threat detection, incident response, and mitigation strategies to safeguard systems and networks against evolving cyber threats.

Chapter 7: Database Forensics

SQL database forensics involves the systematic investigation and analysis of SQL (Structured Query Language) databases to uncover evidence of malicious activities, data breaches, unauthorized access, or data manipulation. The process begins with **Database Identification**, where forensic analysts identify SQL databases (`mysql -u root -p`) on a system using commands like `mysql -u root -p`, prompting for the root user password (`-p`) to log in and access MySQL databases.

Database Examination techniques involve extracting and examining database schemas (`SHOW DATABASES;`) and tables (`USE database_name; SHOW TABLES;`), using SQL queries (`SHOW DATABASES;`, `USE database_name; SHOW TABLES;`) to list available databases and navigate through tables within the MySQL environment.

Data Recovery methods focus on recovering deleted or modified records (`SELECT * FROM table_name;`), executing SQL queries (`SELECT * FROM table_name;`) to retrieve (`SELECT * FROM table_name;`) data from specific tables (`table_name`) within the database.

Transaction Log Analysis involves examining transaction logs (`fn_dblog()`) using SQL Server Management Studio (`fn_dblog();`), executing commands like `fn_dblog();` to view (`fn_dblog()`) transaction log details (`fn_dblog()`) such as transactions, operations, and timestamps (`fn_dblog()`).

Forensic Imaging of SQL databases involves creating a bit-by-bit copy (`dd`) of database files (`dd if=/dev/sda of=forensic_image.dd`), using commands like `dd if=/dev/sda of=forensic_image.dd` to image (`dd`) SQL database files (`if=/dev/sda`) for forensic analysis (`of=forensic_image.dd`).

Database Reconstruction techniques involve reconstructing (`reconstruct database_name`) databases (`reconstruct database_name`) from acquired data (`database_name`) using database management tools (`reconstruct database_name`).

Metadata Analysis involves examining (`EXTRACTVALUE()`) metadata (`EXTRACTVALUE()`) embedded in SQL databases (`EXTRACTVALUE()`) using SQL queries (`EXTRACTVALUE()`) to extract specific values (`EXTRACTVALUE()`) such as creation dates (`EXTRACTVALUE()`) and database configurations (`EXTRACTVALUE()`).

Query Analysis involves analyzing (`EXPLAIN`) SQL queries (`EXPLAIN SELECT * FROM table_name;`) using SQL commands (`EXPLAIN SELECT * FROM table_name;`) to optimize (`EXPLAIN`) query execution (`SELECT * FROM table_name;`) and identify performance issues (`EXPLAIN`).

Backup Analysis techniques involve examining (`RESTORE DATABASE database_name`) and analyzing (`RESTORE DATABASE database_name`) SQL database backups (`RESTORE DATABASE database_name`) to retrieve (`RESTORE DATABASE database_name`) data (`database_name`).

Data Validation involves verifying (`CHECKDB database_name`) data (`CHECKDB database_name`) integrity

(`CHECKDB database_name`) using SQL Server Management Studio (`CHECKDB database_name`).

Query Reconstruction involves reconstructing (`REPAIR TABLE table_name`) SQL queries (`REPAIR TABLE table_name`) using SQL commands (`REPAIR TABLE table_name`) to repair (`REPAIR TABLE table_name`) database (`table_name`) tables (`REPAIR TABLE table_name`).

Forensic Reporting includes preparing comprehensive (`REPORT database_name`) reports (`REPORT database_name`) summarizing (`REPORT database_name`) findings (`REPORT database_name`) and analysis (`REPORT database_name`) using SQL queries (`REPORT database_name`).

In summary, SQL database forensics encompasses a wide array of techniques and methodologies (`SELECT * FROM table_name;`) to investigate (`SELECT * FROM table_name;`) and analyze (`SELECT * FROM table_name;`) SQL databases (`SELECT * FROM table_name;`) for forensic (`SELECT * FROM table_name;`) purposes (`SELECT * FROM table_name;`). These techniques (`SELECT * FROM table_name;`) are crucial (`SELECT * FROM table_name;`) for identifying (`SELECT * FROM table_name;`) and mitigating (`SELECT * FROM table_name;`) security breaches (`SELECT * FROM table_name;`) and ensuring data (`SELECT * FROM table_name;`) integrity (`SELECT * FROM table_name;`) and compliance (`SELECT * FROM table_name;`) within SQL (`SELECT * FROM table_name;`) database (`SELECT * FROM table_name;`) environments.

NoSQL database forensics is a specialized field within digital forensics that focuses on investigating and analyzing NoSQL

(Not only SQL) databases to uncover evidence of cyber incidents, data breaches, unauthorized access, or data manipulation. The process starts with **Database Identification**, where forensic analysts identify NoSQL databases (`mongo`) on a system using commands like `mongo`, which opens the MongoDB shell, allowing access to databases and collections (`show dbs`, `use database_name`).

Database Schema Examination involves examining the structure of NoSQL databases (`db.collection.findOne()`) and their collections (`db.collection.findOne()`), using commands such as `db.collection.findOne()` to retrieve a document from a collection (`db.collection.findOne()`) within the database (`db.collection.findOne()`).

Data Recovery methods focus on recovering deleted or modified records (`db.collection.find()`), executing queries (`db.collection.find()`) to retrieve data (`db.collection.find()`) from specific collections (`db.collection.find()`).

Transaction Log Analysis includes analyzing (`rs.printReplicationInfo()`) replication information (`rs.printReplicationInfo()`) in MongoDB (`rs.printReplicationInfo()`), revealing details about data changes (`rs.printReplicationInfo()`) across replica sets (`rs.printReplicationInfo()`).

Forensic Imaging of NoSQL databases involves creating a backup (`mongodump`) of database (`mongodump --db database_name`) data (`mongodump`) using commands like `mongodump --db database_name`, which exports (`mongodump`) MongoDB (`--db database_name`) database (`mongodump --db database_name`) data (`--db database_name`).

Metadata Analysis entails examining (`db.collection.getIndexes()`) indexes (`db.collection.getIndexes()`) in MongoDB collections (`db.collection.getIndexes()`), revealing index information (`db.collection.getIndexes()`) and usage (`db.collection.getIndexes()`).

Query Analysis involves analyzing (`explain()`) query execution plans (`explain()`) in MongoDB (`explain()`), using methods like `explain()` to optimize (`explain()`) query performance (`explain()`).

Backup Analysis techniques involve restoring (`mongorestore`) MongoDB backups (`mongorestore --db database_name`) using commands such as `mongorestore --db database_name`, which imports (`mongorestore`) MongoDB (`--db database_name`) backup (`mongorestore --db database_name`) data (`--db database_name`).

Data Validation includes validating (`db.collection.validate()`) MongoDB collections (`db.collection.validate()`), ensuring data (`db.collection.validate()`) consistency and integrity (`db.collection.validate()`).

Query Reconstruction entails reconstructing (`db.collection.reIndex()`) indexes (`db.collection.reIndex()`) in MongoDB collections (`db.collection.reIndex()`), optimizing (`db.collection.reIndex()`) index performance (`db.collection.reIndex()`).

Forensic Reporting involves generating (`db.stats()`) statistics (`db.stats()`) and metrics (`db.stats()`) about MongoDB databases (`db.stats()`), providing insights (`db.stats()`) into database (`db.stats()`) usage and performance (`db.stats()`).

In summary, NoSQL database forensics encompasses a range of techniques and methodologies (`db.collection.find()`) tailored (`db.collection.find()`) for investigating (`db.collection.find()`) and analyzing (`db.collection.find()`) NoSQL (`db.collection.find()`) databases (`db.collection.find()`) in forensic (`db.collection.find()`) investigations. These techniques (`db.collection.find()`) are crucial (`db.collection.find()`) for uncovering (`db.collection.find()`) digital evidence (`db.collection.find()`) and identifying (`db.collection.find()`) security incidents (`db.collection.find()`) within NoSQL (`db.collection.find()`) database (`db.collection.find()`) environments.

Chapter 8: Cloud Forensics

Investigating cloud service providers is a critical aspect of modern digital forensics, necessitating thorough understanding and adept use of forensic techniques tailored specifically for cloud environments. Cloud service providers (CSPs) offer vast computing resources and storage capabilities over the internet, posing unique challenges and opportunities for forensic investigators. **Initial Identification** of relevant CSPs involves determining which providers (`aws s3 ls`) may have been involved in hosting (`aws s3 ls`) or processing (`aws s3 ls`) data relevant to the investigation (`aws s3 ls`).

Legal and Administrative Considerations include understanding the jurisdiction (`aws s3 cp`) and compliance (`aws s3 cp`) requirements (`aws s3 cp`) associated with accessing (`aws s3 cp`) and analyzing (`aws s3 cp`) data stored (`aws s3 cp`) in cloud environments (`aws s3 cp`).

Data Collection from cloud services (`aws s3 sync`) requires techniques (`aws s3 sync`) for securely (`aws s3 sync`) gathering (`aws s3 sync`) evidence (`aws s3 sync`) without compromising (`aws s3 sync`) its integrity (`aws s3 sync`).

Incident Response Planning for cloud environments (`aws s3 mv`) involves developing (`aws s3 mv`) strategies (`aws s3 mv`) and procedures (`aws s3 mv`) to swiftly (`aws s3 mv`) respond (`aws s3 mv`) to security incidents (`aws s3 mv`) and data breaches (`aws s3 mv`).

Forensic Imaging of cloud instances (`aws ec2 create-image`) ensures (`aws ec2 create-image`) preservation (`aws ec2 create-image`) of volatile (`aws ec2 create-image`) digital evidence (`aws ec2 create-image`) for subsequent (`aws ec2 create-image`) analysis (`aws ec2 create-image`).

Metadata Analysis (`aws s3api list-objects`) involves examining (`aws s3api list-objects`) object (`aws s3api list-objects`) metadata (`aws s3api list-objects`) to glean (`aws s3api list-objects`) insights (`aws s3api list-objects`) into file (`aws s3api list-objects`) creation (`aws s3api list-objects`) dates (`aws s3api list-objects`) and access patterns (`aws s3api list-objects`).

Network Traffic Analysis (`aws logs get-log-events`) helps (`aws logs get-log-events`) identify (`aws logs get-log-events`) potential (`aws logs get-log-events`) unauthorized (`aws logs get-log-events`) access (`aws logs get-log-events`) or data (`aws logs get-log-events`) exfiltration (`aws logs get-log-events`).

Database Forensics (`aws rds describe-db-instances`) focuses on examining (`aws rds describe-db-instances`) databases (`aws rds describe-db-instances`) hosted (`aws rds describe-db-instances`) in cloud (`aws rds describe-db-instances`) instances (`aws rds describe-db-instances`).

Malware Analysis (`aws lambda invoke`) within cloud (`aws lambda invoke`) functions (`aws lambda invoke`) aids (`aws lambda invoke`) in identifying (`aws lambda invoke`) and mitigating (`aws lambda invoke`) potential (`aws lambda invoke`) threats (`aws lambda invoke`).

Logging and Monitoring (`aws cloudtrail describe-trails`) play (`aws cloudtrail describe-trails`) a pivotal (`aws cloudtrail describe-trails`) role (`aws cloudtrail describe-trails`) in tracking (`aws cloudtrail describe-trails`) and auditing (`aws cloudtrail describe-trails`) activities (`aws cloudtrail describe-trails`) within cloud (`aws cloudtrail describe-trails`) environments (`aws cloudtrail describe-trails`).

Digital Evidence Handling (`aws kms encrypt`) adheres (`aws kms encrypt`) to protocols (`aws kms encrypt`) for securely (`aws kms encrypt`) storing (`aws kms encrypt`) and transferring (`aws kms encrypt`) forensic (`aws kms encrypt`) data (`aws kms encrypt`).

Documentation and Reporting (`aws s3api put-object`) ensure (`aws s3api put-object`) comprehensive (`aws s3api put-object`) documentation (`aws s3api put-object`) of findings (`aws s3api put-object`) and actions (`aws s3api put-object`) taken (`aws s3api put-object`).

Continuous Improvement (`aws config get-compliance-details-by-config-rule`) involves refining (`aws config get-compliance-details-by-config-rule`) incident response (`aws config get-compliance-details-by-config-rule`) processes (`aws config get-compliance-details-by-config-rule`) based (`aws config get-compliance-details-by-config-rule`) on lessons (`aws config get-compliance-details-by-config-rule`) learned (`aws config get-compliance-details-by-config-rule`) from each investigation (`aws config get-compliance-details-by-config-rule`).

In summary, investigating cloud service providers (`aws s3api list-buckets`) requires (`aws s3api list-buckets`) a holistic (`aws s3api list-buckets`) approach (`aws s3api list-buckets`) integrating (`aws s3api list-buckets`) technical (`aws s3api list-buckets`) expertise (`aws s3api list-buckets`) with legal (`aws s3api list-buckets`) considerations (`aws s3api list-buckets`) to effectively (`aws s3api list-buckets`) address (`aws s3api list-buckets`) cybersecurity (`aws s3api list-buckets`) challenges (`aws s3api list-buckets`) in cloud (`aws s3api list-buckets`) environments (`aws s3api list-buckets`).Recovering data from cloud environments is a crucial aspect of digital forensics, necessitating specialized techniques tailored for the unique architecture and storage mechanisms of cloud service providers (CSPs). Cloud environments offer vast scalability and flexibility, allowing organizations to store and process data remotely, which poses distinct challenges and opportunities for forensic investigators (`aws s3 ls`). Understanding the structure and deployment (`aws s3 ls`) of data within a specific CSP (`aws s3 ls`) is fundamental (`aws s3 ls`) to successful (`aws s3 ls`) data recovery (`aws s3 ls`). **Legal and Compliance Considerations** (`aws s3 cp`) must be meticulously (`aws s3 cp`) navigated (`aws s3 cp`) to ensure (`aws s3 cp`) adherence (`aws s3 cp`) to relevant (`aws s3 cp`) regulations (`aws s3 cp`) and privacy (`aws s3 cp`) requirements (`aws s3 cp`).

Initial Assessment (`aws s3 cp`) involves identifying (`aws s3 cp`) the scope (`aws s3 cp`) and nature (`aws s3 cp`) of data loss (`aws s3 cp`) or corruption (`aws s3 cp`), determining (`aws s3 cp`) whether the data (`aws s3 cp`) resides (`aws s3 cp`) in object (`aws s3 cp`) storage (`aws s3 cp`), databases (`aws s3 cp`), or other (`aws s3 cp`) cloud (`aws s3 cp`) services (`aws s3 cp`). **Data Collection** (`aws s3 sync`) methods (`aws s3 sync`) must be chosen (`aws s3 sync`) based (`aws s3 sync`) on the type (`aws s3 sync`) and location (`aws s3 sync`) of the data (`aws s3 sync`), ensuring (`aws s3 sync`) integrity (`aws s3 sync`) and chain of custody (`aws s3 sync`) are maintained (`aws s3 sync`) throughout (`aws s3 sync`) the process (`aws s3 sync`).

Forensic Imaging (`aws ec2 create-image`) of cloud (`aws ec2 create-image`) instances (`aws ec2 create-image`) may be necessary (`aws ec2 create-image`) to preserve (`aws ec2 create-image`) volatile (`aws ec2 create-image`) evidence (`aws ec2 create-image`) and facilitate (`aws ec2 create-image`) offline (`aws ec2 create-image`) analysis (`aws ec2 create-image`). **Metadata Analysis** (`aws s3api list-objects`) plays (`aws s3api list-objects`) a crucial (`aws s3api list-objects`) role (`aws s3api list-objects`) in understanding (`aws s3api list-objects`) the context (`aws s3api list-objects`) and usage (`aws s3api list-objects`) patterns (`aws s3api list-objects`) of the data (`aws s3api list-objects`) within (`aws s3api list-objects`) the cloud (`aws s3api list-objects`) environment (`aws s3api list-objects`).

Network Traffic Analysis (`aws logs get-log-events`) and **Access Logs** (`aws cloudtrail describe-trails`) can (`aws cloudtrail describe-trails`) provide (`aws cloudtrail describe-trails`) insights (`aws cloudtrail describe-trails`) into potential (`aws cloudtrail describe-trails`) unauthorized (`aws cloudtrail describe-trails`) access (`aws cloudtrail describe-trails`) or data (`aws cloudtrail describe-trails`) exfiltration (`aws cloudtrail describe-trails`). **Database Forensics** (`aws rds describe-db-instances`) techniques (`aws rds describe-db-instances`) are essential (`aws rds describe-db-instances`) for analyzing (`aws rds describe-db-instances`) data (`aws rds describe-db-instances`) stored (`aws rds describe-db-instances`) in cloud (`aws rds describe-db-instances`) databases (`aws rds describe-db-instances`).

Malware Analysis (`aws lambda invoke`) and **Endpoint Forensics** (`aws inspector list-findings`) might (`aws inspector list-findings`) be necessary (`aws inspector list-findings`) to identify (`aws inspector list-findings`) and mitigate (`aws inspector list-findings`) security (`aws inspector list-findings`) risks (`aws inspector list-findings`) within (`aws inspector list-findings`) the cloud (`aws inspector list-findings`) environment (`aws inspector list-findings`). **Log Analysis** (`aws logs filter-log-events`) and **Anomaly Detection** (`aws guardduty list-detectors`) techniques (`aws guardduty list-detectors`) can (`aws guardduty list-detectors`) help (`aws guardduty list-detectors`) in detecting (`aws guardduty list-detectors`) suspicious (`aws guardduty list-detectors`) activities (`aws guardduty list-detectors`) or events (`aws guardduty list-detectors`) that (`aws guardduty list-detectors`) may (`aws guardduty list-detectors`) indicate (`aws guardduty list-detectors`) a data (`aws guardduty list-detectors`) breach (`aws guardduty list-detectors`).

Documentation and Reporting (`aws s3api put-object`) throughout (`aws s3api put-object`) the recovery (`aws s3api put-object`) process (`aws s3api put-object`) are crucial (`aws s3api put-object`) for maintaining (`aws s3api put-object`) a clear (`aws s3api put-object`) record (`aws s3api put-object`) of actions (`aws s3api put-object`) taken (`aws s3api put-object`) and findings (`aws s3api put-object`). **Continuous Improvement** (`aws config get-compliance-details-by-config-rule`) involves (`aws config get-compliance-details-by-config-rule`) refining (`aws config get-compliance-details-by-config-rule`) incident response (`aws config get-compliance-details-by-config-rule`) procedures (`aws config get-compliance-details-by-config-rule`) based (`aws config get-compliance-details-by-config-rule`) on lessons (`aws config get-compliance-details-by-config-rule`) learned (`aws config get-compliance-details-by-config-rule`) from each recovery (`aws config get-compliance-details-by-config-rule`) effort (`aws config get-compliance-details-by-config-rule`).

In summary, recovering (`aws s3 cp`) data from cloud (`aws s3 cp`) environments (`aws s3 cp`) demands (`aws s3 cp`) a meticulous (`aws s3 cp`) approach (`aws s3 cp`) that (`aws s3 cp`) integrates (`aws s3 cp`) technical (`aws s3 cp`) expertise (`aws s3 cp`) with legal (`aws s3 cp`) awareness (`aws s3 cp`) and compliance (`aws s3 cp`) considerations (`aws s3 cp`) to ensure (`aws s3 cp`) effective (`aws s3 cp`) and thorough (`aws s3 cp`) forensic (`aws s3 cp`) investigations (`aws s3 cp`).

Chapter 9: Incident Response Automation and Orchestration

In the realm of cybersecurity, the complexity and frequency of incidents have necessitated the development of more sophisticated response mechanisms. Incident response automation and orchestration are critical components in the modern cybersecurity landscape, enabling organizations to effectively manage and mitigate threats. Automation involves using technology to perform tasks without human intervention, while orchestration integrates and coordinates multiple automated tasks to work seamlessly together.

One of the foundational elements of incident response automation is the use of Security Information and Event Management (SIEM) systems. SIEM solutions collect and analyze security data from various sources within an organization's network, providing real-time insights and alerts. When a potential security incident is detected, automated workflows can be triggered to initiate a series of predefined actions. For instance, if a SIEM system identifies an unusual login attempt from a foreign IP address, it can automatically trigger a script to block the IP and notify the security team. A common command for viewing real-time logs in a SIEM system might be `tail -f /var/log/syslog`.

Integrating Threat Intelligence Platforms (TIPs) into the incident response framework enhances the automation process. TIPs aggregate threat data from various sources, enabling the automation system to make informed decisions based on the latest threat intelligence. For example, when a new threat is identified, the TIP can update the SIEM system's rules to detect similar threats, automatically adjusting the organization's defenses. To update threat intelligence feeds, a command such as `curl -X GET https://api.threatintel.com/feed/update -H "Authorization: Bearer API_KEY"` can be used.

Incident response playbooks are essential tools for defining the steps to be taken during various types of incidents. These playbooks outline specific actions to be performed in response to specific triggers. By automating these steps, organizations can ensure a consistent and rapid response to incidents. For instance, a playbook for handling a phishing attack might include steps such as isolating the affected systems, collecting forensic data, and resetting user credentials. Automating these steps can be achieved using scripts and orchestration tools. A simple automation script to reset user passwords might include the command `passwd username`.

The orchestration of incident response activities involves coordinating multiple automated tasks across different systems and tools. Orchestration platforms, such as Security Orchestration, Automation, and

Response (SOAR) solutions, play a crucial role in this process. SOAR platforms integrate with various security tools, enabling automated workflows that span different systems. For instance, a SOAR platform can orchestrate a response to a malware infection by coordinating actions between the SIEM system, antivirus software, and network firewalls. This might involve commands such as `systemctl stop malware-service`, `clamscan -r /home/user`, and `iptables -A INPUT -s malicious_ip -j DROP`.

Automation and orchestration not only improve the speed and efficiency of incident response but also reduce the likelihood of human error. By automating repetitive tasks, security teams can focus on more complex and strategic activities. For example, automated malware analysis can quickly identify and categorize malware, freeing up analysts to focus on threat hunting and investigating sophisticated attacks. To perform an automated malware analysis, a command like `malware_analysis_tool --scan /path/to/file` can be used.

A key aspect of successful incident response automation is ensuring that all automated actions are thoroughly tested and regularly updated. This includes validating that scripts and workflows function as intended and do not inadvertently disrupt normal operations. Testing can be conducted in a controlled environment, often referred to as a sandbox, where automated actions can be safely executed without impacting live systems. A command to run a script in a sandbox environment might look like `sandbox_exec /path/to/script`.

Integration with ticketing systems is another important component of incident response automation. When an incident is detected, automated workflows can create and update tickets in the organization's ticketing system, ensuring that all relevant information is documented and tracked. This helps maintain a clear audit trail and facilitates effective communication within the security team. To create a ticket automatically, a command such as `curl -X POST https://api.ticketing.com/tickets -d '{"title":"Incident Detected","description":"Details of the incident"}' -H "Authorization: Bearer API_KEY"` can be used.

Moreover, automated reporting and notification systems are essential for keeping stakeholders informed about ongoing incidents. These systems can generate detailed incident reports and send notifications to relevant personnel via email, SMS, or other communication channels. Automating these processes ensures that critical information is disseminated promptly, enabling faster decision-making. A command to send an email notification might include `echo "Incident report" | mail -s "Incident Alert" team@company.com`.

Another critical element of incident response automation is the use of machine learning and artificial intelligence (AI) to enhance detection and response capabilities. Machine learning algorithms can analyze vast amounts of security data to identify patterns and anomalies that might indicate a security incident. These insights can then be used to trigger automated responses. For example, an AI-based system might detect an unusual increase in network traffic indicative of a DDoS attack and automatically initiate mitigation actions. Training a machine learning model for this purpose might involve a command like `python train_model.py --data /path/to/training/data`.

Incident response automation also extends to the post-incident analysis phase. Automated tools can collect and analyze data from the incident to identify root causes and recommend improvements to the organization's security posture. This continuous improvement process helps organizations become more resilient to future attacks. For instance, an automated post-incident analysis tool might generate a report with a command such as `incident_analysis_tool --incident_id 12345 --output report.pdf`.

Incorporating automation and orchestration into incident response strategies requires careful planning and consideration of various factors, including the organization's specific needs, existing security infrastructure, and the expertise of the security team. It is essential to strike a balance between automation and human oversight, ensuring that automated actions are aligned with the organization's security policies and procedures. To deploy an automation script securely, one might use a command like `ansible-playbook -i hosts deploy_automation.yml`.

Overall, incident response automation and orchestration significantly enhance an organization's ability to detect, respond to, and recover from security incidents. By leveraging advanced technologies and integrating various security tools and processes, organizations can achieve a more proactive and effective security posture. This not only helps mitigate the impact of incidents but also improves the overall efficiency and effectiveness of the security team. As the threat landscape continues to evolve, the importance of automation and orchestration in incident response will only grow, making it a vital component of any comprehensive cybersecurity strategy.

Chapter 10: Forensic Reporting and Expert Witness Testimony

Writing effective forensic reports is a critical skill for forensic professionals, encompassing clarity, precision, and the ability to convey complex information in an understandable manner, which is essential not only for the sake of legal proceedings but also for ensuring the information is accessible to non-experts, including jurors and legal teams; the primary goal is to present all relevant facts and analyses without bias, ensuring that the report stands up to scrutiny both in and out of a courtroom. To begin, it's crucial to structure the report logically, starting with a clear title and a table of contents if the report is lengthy, and each section should be clearly numbered and titled to guide the reader through the document; the executive summary follows, which should encapsulate the key findings and conclusions succinctly, providing a snapshot of the report's contents for those who may not delve into the full document. Detailed findings should be discussed in their own sections, each dedicated to a specific aspect of the investigation, such as evidence collection, laboratory analysis, and interpretation of results; it's important to use subheadings and bullet points to break up text and make the information more digestible, especially when explaining technical processes or complex data. Visual aids like charts, graphs, and photographs can significantly enhance the comprehensibility of the report, illustrating key points and providing visual proof that complements the written text; these should be clearly labeled and referenced in the text, explaining exactly what they depict and why they are relevant. When dealing with digital evidence, for example, screenshots or system logs might be crucial, and you should include commands used during digital forensic investigations to collect or analyze evidence, such as `dd if=/dev/sda of=/path/to/image.img bs=4096 conv=noerror,sync` to create a bit-for-bit image of a drive, or `grep -i 'keyword' /path/to/file` to search for specific terms within a file system, ensuring these commands are written out fully to avoid ambiguity and provide a clear, traceable methodology. Furthermore, it is imperative to explain all technical terms and jargon; a glossary can be included at the end of the report to define terms such as 'hash value' or 'MAC address', which ensures that the report is accessible to those without technical backgrounds. The analysis section is where the forensic expert's skills are showcased, detailing how conclusions were drawn from the data; this should be methodical and evidence-backed, citing software tools used, versions, and settings, for instance, mentioning the use of tools like EnCase or Autopsy for data recovery and analysis, specifying the software settings and processes followed, which provides transparency and reproducibility of the forensic examination. It's also crucial to remain objective and refrain from drawing conclusions without sufficient evidence; if uncertainties or ambiguities in the data exist, these must be clearly stated, avoiding the temptation to speculate beyond the evidence. The report should end with a concise conclusion that ties together all sections, summarizing the evidence and findings without introducing any new information, and should be followed by an appendix section if additional documentation or raw data is necessary to support the report's findings. Throughout the report, maintaining a formal tone and using passive voice can help preserve objectivity, focusing on the actions taken rather than the individual performing them, and attention to detail is paramount, ensuring that every statement can be substantiated and every piece of evidence is duly noted and correctly cited, using consistent and precise referencing styles. Finally, before finalizing the report, a thorough review is essential to catch any errors, ambiguities, or omissions; peer reviews or consultations with other experts in the field can provide an additional layer of scrutiny, helping to refine the report and ensure it meets the high standards required for forensic documentation. Preparing for expert witness testimony requires a deep understanding of both the technical aspects of the subject matter and the legal context in which the testimony will be delivered, making thorough preparation pivotal; the expert must become intimately familiar with all details of the case, reviewing all relevant documents, evidence, and any prior depositions related to the matter, and this includes technical reports, witness statements, and any other evidence gathered during the investigation, as well as understanding the legal standards and the burden of proof that apply to the case. It is essential for the expert to prepare by practicing clear and concise communication, focusing on explaining complex technical matters in a way that is accessible to those without a specialized background, such as jurors or judges, who may not be familiar with the technical jargon; this might involve simplifying explanations without losing the accuracy or scientific integrity of the information, a skill that can be honed through mock trials and rehearsal sessions with legal counsel. During these sessions, the expert can receive feedback on their delivery and content, learning how to frame their testimony to make it as clear and effective as possible, while also preparing to handle cross-examination, which often involves challenging questions aimed at discrediting the expert's findings or character; effective preparation includes developing responses to potential questions that may be posed by opposing counsel, ensuring the expert remains composed and maintains their credibility throughout the process. Additionally, understanding the rules of the courtroom and the specific procedures of the court in which they will be testifying is crucial; this includes familiarizing themselves with any limitations on testimony, such as time constraints or evidentiary rules that may impact what can be said or how information can be presented. Part of the preparation also involves ensuring all technical tools and demonstrations are ready and functioning, such as slide presentations or video displays, which must be tested in advance to avoid technical difficulties during the testimony; experts should also prepare all necessary documentation, such as charts, graphs, or models, which can help illustrate their points more effectively during their testimony. Furthermore, it is advisable to review similar past cases or literature to understand how particular issues have been addressed or interpreted by the courts in the past, which can provide valuable insights into potential legal arguments or points of contention. Experts must also ensure they adhere to ethical standards, avoiding any potential conflicts of interest and remaining unbiased and objective in their testimony; this includes disclosing any material interests or relationships that could be seen as compromising their impartiality. Finally, close coordination with the legal team is essential to align the expert's contributions with the broader strategy of the case, ensuring that their testimony effectively supports the case objectives and responds appropriately to the issues raised by the opposition, with the expert and legal team reviewing the main themes and strategies regularly to ensure consistency and readiness for the day of testimony.

BOOK 3
ADVANCED COUNTERINTELLIGENCE STRATEGIES:
EXPERT METHODS IN CYBER INCIDENT RESPONSE

ROB BOTWRIGHT

Chapter 1: Advanced Threat Intelligence Gathering

Open Source Intelligence (OSINT) techniques harness publicly available sources to gather and analyze information, making it a critical tool for researchers, security analysts, and intelligence agencies, which involves several methodologies and tools designed to extract, collate, and analyze data from various open sources such as media, public government data, professional and academic publications, and more; one of the first techniques in OSINT involves defining the intelligence requirements clearly which guides the data collection process, ensuring that the information gathered is relevant and useful. Once the objectives are defined, data collection can begin by using tools like search engines, social media platforms, websites, and other internet-based resources, and advanced search operators such as `site:`, `filetype:`, and `intext:` can be used to refine search results in Google, improving the precision of the data collected. For example, `filetype:pdf intext:"confidential" site:example.com` will search for PDF files containing the word "confidential" within the domain "example.com". Social media platforms are also invaluable for OSINT, with tools like TweetDeck or Twint allowing users to monitor tweets and hashtags in real-time or perform advanced searches on Twitter without using the API; for instance, running the command `twint -u username --since 2020-01-01 --until 2020-01-31 -o output.csv --csv` collects tweets from a specific user between specified dates and outputs them to a CSV file. Additionally, geolocation tools and satellite imagery can provide insights into the physical locations and environments, which are crucial for investigations involving movements or changes in specific areas; tools like Google Earth or Wikimapia offer detailed satellite views and can be supplemented with historical imagery data to observe changes over time. Another key OSINT technique involves the use of data scraping tools to automate the collection of data from websites, which is especially useful when dealing with large volumes of information; Python libraries such as Beautiful Soup and Scrapy are widely used for this purpose, where Beautiful Soup allows for easy extraction of data from HTML and XML files using commands like `soup.findAll('a')` to find all hyperlinks on a webpage. Analyzing the collected data is another critical phase where the information is sorted, verified, and analyzed to identify patterns, connections, and insights; tools like Maltego can be used for link analysis, providing a graphical representation of relationships and connections between people, groups, and organizations based on the data collected. Furthermore, the OSINT cycle is iterative, meaning analysts often need to refine their search parameters and collection methods as new information and insights are gained, ensuring the intelligence remains accurate and up-to-date. To maintain operational security and anonymity while conducting OSINT research, tools like Tor and VPNs are essential, protecting the researcher's identity and location from potential adversaries. Moreover, maintaining a legal and ethical approach during OSINT operations is paramount to ensure compliance with laws and regulations, especially concerning data protection and privacy; therefore, analysts must stay informed about legal constraints and ethical considerations related to the collection and use of data from public sources. Finally, documenting the entire OSINT process meticulously is crucial for transparency and for providing context to the findings, which involves keeping detailed records of sources, search queries, and methodologies used throughout the investigation, thus allowing the analysis to be reproducible and verifiable by other researchers or stakeholders involved in the process. Dark web monitoring and analysis involve the exploration and assessment of hidden online spaces, primarily accessible through tools like Tor (The Onion Router), which anonymize user identities and locations, a critical technique for cybersecurity experts, law enforcement agencies, and intelligence professionals seeking to uncover illicit activities without revealing their tracks; starting with the installation of Tor, which can be done by downloading the Tor browser from the official website, users can access .onion domains that are not indexed by conventional search engines, with these sites often hosting forums, marketplaces, and blogs that deal in everything from cybersecurity threats to illegal commodities. Once on the dark web, it's crucial to employ secure practices to avoid detection and ensure safety; this includes disabling JavaScript, not downloading files or enabling scripts, and using virtual machines to isolate browsing activity from critical systems. For monitoring purposes, tools like Ahmia.fi provide search capabilities across .onion sites, helping users to find specific content or investigate dark web site availability, and another valuable tool for dark web analysis is OnionScan, which scans .onion sites for security vulnerabilities, operational security issues, and configuration errors by simply executing the command `onionscan -scans web <.onion URL>`. Advanced techniques involve setting up automated crawlers that can systematically explore dark web sites to collect data over time, using Python scripts with libraries like `requests` and `bs4` to automate the fetching and parsing of HTML content from dark web pages, for example, deploying a script that periodically checks for changes in content or new listings on specific marketplaces, which can provide insights into trends and emerging threats in the cybercrime landscape. Analysts often employ data analysis tools to sift through collected data, using software like Maltego for link analysis or Elasticsearch for managing and querying large datasets, where data can be visualized and examined to reveal hidden patterns, connections, and intelligence insights that can guide cybersecurity measures or law enforcement actions. Furthermore, blockchain analysis is also a part of dark web monitoring, particularly relevant for tracing cryptocurrency transactions, which are commonly used for payments on the dark web; tools like Chainalysis and WalletExplorer can be used to track these transactions, linking them to specific wallets and potentially identifying the parties involved if the wallets can be associated with real-world identities. The information collected through dark web monitoring must be handled with caution, respecting privacy laws and ethical standards, especially considering the anonymity that dark web users expect, thus analysts must ensure that their monitoring activities are justified and lawful, obtaining necessary permissions when required and focusing solely on publicly available information or information pertinent to specific investigations. Regular updates and training are necessary to keep up with the evolving nature of dark web technologies and the shifting landscape of online threats, ensuring that monitoring techniques remain effective and that tools are updated to circumvent any new security measures implemented by dark web sites. Collaboration and information sharing among various stakeholders, including cybersecurity firms, government agencies, and international organizations, can enhance the effectiveness of dark web monitoring efforts, pooling resources and knowledge to tackle the challenges posed by the anonymity and lawlessness often found in these hidden corners of the internet. Finally, documenting all findings and methods in detailed reports helps maintain a clear audit trail of activities and supports accountability and transparency in dark web operations, ensuring that all actions are traceable and grounded in robust analysis and lawful practice.

Chapter 2: Cyber Threat Modeling and Risk Assessment

Threat actor profiling and attribution involve the detailed analysis of cyber attacks to identify and understand the perpetrators, a critical component of cybersecurity which helps organizations develop targeted defense strategies and potentially take legal action against the attackers; the process begins with the collection of digital artifacts from security breaches, such as malware samples, system logs, network traffic, and phishing emails, which are then scrutinized to extract indicators of compromise (IOCs) that can be used to trace the origins of the attack. Tools like VirusTotal or Hybrid Analysis allow analysts to submit suspicious files or URLs and receive reports detailing their behavior, relationships, and other artifacts linked to known threat actors, while the use of sandbox environments to execute and observe malware can reveal additional information about the attackers' techniques and objectives, for instance running `cuckoo submit --package exe <malware_sample>` in Cuckoo Sandbox to analyze a Windows executable file. Once the data is collected, correlation and analysis are performed using Security Information and Event Management (SIEM) systems, which aggregate and analyze logs and alerts from various sources within an organization to identify patterns and anomalies that might indicate a coordinated attack; for example, using a SIEM tool like Splunk with a command like `index=firewall | stats count by src_ip, dest_ip` can help identify unusual traffic patterns or potential command and control (C2) servers. Behavioral analysis extends to understanding the tactics, techniques, and procedures (TTPs) of the attackers, which are compared against known threat actor profiles in databases such as MITRE ATT&CK, a globally accessible knowledge base of adversary tactics and techniques based on real-world observations, where analysts can match attack patterns to previously documented cases to hypothesize the likely perpetrators. Advanced threat actor profiling may also involve the study of the socio-political context or the language used in attack codes or communications, which can suggest the nationality or motivation of the attackers, and in cases where attackers communicate directly, such as in ransomware cases, the analysis of language style and demands can provide crucial clues about their identity and location. Cyber threat intelligence (CTI) feeds play a pivotal role in this process by providing up-to-date information about new and emerging threats, which helps organizations to stay ahead of attackers and adjust their security measures accordingly; such feeds often include details about new malware variants, IP addresses linked to malicious activity, and updates on the tactics employed by specific threat actors, which can be integrated into threat intelligence platforms to enhance ongoing monitoring and analysis efforts. Furthermore, collaboration with external entities such as other affected organizations, cybersecurity firms, and law enforcement can greatly enhance the accuracy and depth of threat actor profiling by pooling resources and sharing insights, which not only improves the chances of successful attribution but also helps build a more comprehensive defense against future attacks. Attribution, while challenging, involves confirming the identity of the attackers, which is often complicated by techniques such as IP spoofing, VPNs, and the use of compromised systems as proxies to mask the attackers' true location and identity; nevertheless, persistent and collaborative efforts can sometimes pierce through these obfuscations, particularly when combined with human intelligence (HUMINT) and signals intelligence (SIGINT) that might be available to government agencies. Effective threat actor profiling and attribution require continuous improvement and adaptation of analytical techniques to keep pace with the evolving nature of cyber threats, and while complete certainty in attribution might not always be possible, the insights gained through these efforts are invaluable for enhancing security postures and preparing for potential future incidents, ultimately contributing to a proactive cybersecurity strategy that prioritizes understanding and mitigating threats before they can cause significant damage. Risk assessment methodologies provide structured approaches to identifying, analyzing, and managing risks, key to maintaining organizational resilience and ensuring robust risk management strategies; these methodologies typically begin with the identification of potential risks, which involves cataloging possible threats and vulnerabilities that could negatively impact the organization, ranging from cybersecurity threats and technological failures to natural disasters and regulatory changes. The next step is to analyze these risks to determine their likelihood and potential impact, a process that often involves both qualitative and quantitative assessments; quantitative methods may include using formulas to calculate risk scores, such as the Risk = Threat x Vulnerability x Consequence formula, while qualitative methods might involve expert judgment or risk matrices to classify risks as high, medium, or low based on defined criteria. One commonly used methodology is the Failure Modes and Effects Analysis (FMEA), which systematically evaluates potential failure modes within a system to identify their effects on other system components and on the system's ability to achieve the intended functions; executing FMEA involves listing each component, imagining every possible way each component can fail, noting what the consequences of each type of failure could be, and then assessing the severity, occurrence, and detectability of each failure mode, which helps prioritize risk mitigation strategies based on the risk severity and probability. Another widely applied methodology is the Monte Carlo simulation, a statistical technique that uses probability distributions to model and simulate the outcomes of different risks, providing a comprehensive view of potential outcomes and their probabilities; this can be implemented using software like @RISK or custom scripts in programming languages such as Python or R, where random values are generated for uncertain variables to simulate thousands of possible scenarios, helping to predict the likelihood and impact of risk outcomes. The Bowtie method is another technique, visually depicting the relationship between risks, potential causes, and control measures in a bowtie format, which assists in clearly identifying and managing the pathways through which risks can impact an organization, thereby facilitating more effective control and mitigation strategies. For cybersecurity risks, tools such as Nmap or OpenVAS can be utilized to scan systems for vulnerabilities, where commands like `nmap -sV -p 1-65535 -T4 -A -v <target-ip>` are executed to detect open ports and services that might expose the organization to cyber attacks. Risk assessments also incorporate the assessment of residual risk—the risk that remains after controls are applied—and this requires continuous monitoring to ensure that the residual risk remains within acceptable limits; tools like continuous monitoring software or incident response systems can be employed to track the effectiveness of controls and identify when changes or additional measures are necessary. Additionally, risk assessments are iterative processes that must be regularly updated as new threats emerge and as organizational objectives and environments evolve; this involves revisiting and revising risk assessments at regular intervals or when significant changes occur in the operating environment or in the threat landscape. Effective risk management also requires engaging stakeholders across the organization to ensure they understand their roles in managing risks and to ensure that risk management processes are integrated into the organizational culture; training and communication play key roles in this, as they help to align the organization's approach to risk and ensure consistent application of risk assessment methodologies across the enterprise. Furthermore, compliance with legal and regulatory requirements is an integral part of the risk assessment process, requiring organizations to be aware of and comply with relevant laws, regulations, and standards that affect their operational contexts, which can include sector-specific regulations or general data protection laws like the GDPR, impacting how risks are assessed and addressed. Ultimately, the goal of risk assessment methodologies is to provide a proactive, structured, and systematic approach to managing uncertainty, with the aim of minimizing risks while maximizing the ability to achieve organizational objectives, making risk assessment a critical component of strategic management in any organization.

Chapter 3: Advanced Persistent Threat (APT) Investigations

APT TTPs (Tactics, Techniques, and Procedures) analysis focuses on understanding the sophisticated strategies employed by advanced persistent threats (APTs), a type of threat actor typically state-sponsored or highly organized criminals who execute prolonged and targeted cyber attacks to steal data or surveil entities without detection, involving a deep dive into the specifics of how these actors operate, the tools they use, and the sequences of actions they follow to achieve their malicious objectives, thus enabling cybersecurity professionals to anticipate, detect, and mitigate such threats more effectively. To begin with, analysts must collect data regarding incidents that are suspected of being part of an APT campaign, which often involves gathering logs, malware samples, and other artifacts from affected systems using forensic tools like Volatility for memory analysis, where commands such as `volatility -f memorydump.img --profile=Win7SP1x64 pslist` help identify malicious processes that were running on a compromised machine. After data collection, the analysis phase involves dissecting the behavior of the malware or tools used by the threat actors; for instance, tools like IDA Pro or Ghidra can be employed to perform reverse engineering on binaries to uncover their functionality and any built-in obfuscation techniques, providing insights into the technical sophistication of the attackers and their capabilities.

Mapping the identified TTPs to frameworks like MITRE ATT&CK enables analysts to categorize and compare these tactics against a comprehensive database of known threat actor behaviors, where each technique or tactic used by an APT group is documented and cross-referenced with mitigation and detection strategies, which are crucial for enhancing defensive measures against similar attacks in the future. For instance, if an APT group is known to leverage spear-phishing as an initial access tactic, organizations can enhance their email filtering technologies and conduct targeted awareness training to mitigate this risk. Behavioral analysis also plays a significant role in APT TTPs analysis, where cybersecurity teams utilize SIEM systems to correlate suspicious activity across their networks and flag anomalies that might suggest an APT intrusion; commands in a SIEM tool might involve setting correlation rules to alert on sequences of actions that match known APT behaviors, such as `alert on sequence(email_received, url_clicked, payload_download)` which detects a potential phishing attempt followed by a malware download. Further deepening the analysis, threat intelligence platforms can be integrated to pull in information about IP addresses, URLs, and file hashes associated with APT groups, allowing for real-time threat intelligence feeds to inform and update the organization's security posture as new data becomes available. Network traffic analysis is another crucial technique, where tools like Wireshark or tcpdump are used to monitor data packets for signs of exfiltration or C2 communication;

commands such as `tcpdump -i eth0 'src host 192.168.1.1 and (dst port 443 or dst port 80)'` can capture packets coming from a suspected internal host to external servers over common web ports, potentially identifying data exfiltration attempts. Additionally, it's vital for organizations to conduct regular security audits and penetration testing to assess the effectiveness of their defenses against APT-like attacks, using tools and techniques that simulate the actions of APT groups to identify vulnerabilities before they can be exploited by actual attackers. As APT groups continually evolve their tactics, so must the methods used to detect and counteract their actions, which necessitates a dynamic and adaptable cybersecurity strategy that not only reacts to current threats but also anticipates future tactics; ongoing training and upskilling of cybersecurity personnel in the latest cybersecurity technologies and threat analysis methodologies are imperative to maintain a defense-in-depth posture that effectively counters the sophisticated nature of APT campaigns. Additionally, collaboration and information sharing among organizations and between private and public sectors can enhance collective defense capabilities, as insights gained from one attack could potentially prevent another, establishing a community-based defense model that leverages shared knowledge to mitigate the impact of APT activities across the board. APT campaign attribution techniques aim to identify the perpetrators behind advanced persistent threat (APT) activities, a complex process that involves analyzing forensic data, malware samples, and attack patterns to link cyber attacks to specific threat actors or nation-states, which is crucial for understanding the motives, methods, and potential repercussions of cyber espionage or cyber warfare actions; this process begins by collecting all available data related to the intrusion, including system logs, network traffic logs, and any extracted malware artifacts, which are then thoroughly examined using tools like YARA to create rules that help in identifying similar attacks in the future, where a typical command might be `yara -r rules.yara /path/to/suspected/files` to scan a directory of files against known malware signatures. Analysis of malware, often the linchpin in attribution, involves using reverse engineering tools such as Ghidra or IDA Pro to dissect the binary and understand its structure, functionality, and any unique attributes that might link it to known threat actors; for instance, specific malware families are often reused or slightly modified by certain groups, and recognizing these patterns can lead directly to attribution. Network forensics is another critical aspect, focusing on the command and control (C2) infrastructure used by attackers; tools like Wireshark and tcpdump are instrumental here, with commands like `tcpdump -i eth0 'src host 192.168.1.100 and dst port 80' -w output.pcap` to capture packets for later analysis, potentially revealing the origin of traffic or the nature of data being exfiltrated. Leveraging threat intelligence platforms provides additional context, as these platforms aggregate and correlate data on IP addresses, domain names, and other indicators of compromise (IOCs) with known APT groups, enhancing the ability to match observed attack patterns with historical data. Cyber threat intelligence feeds are vital in this respect, offering updates on the latest APT activities and facilitating quicker links between new attacks and known groups. Language analysis, too, plays a role in attribution; examining the language used in phishing emails or malware code comments can provide clues about the nationality or cultural background of the attackers, sometimes even pinpointing specific individuals if unique idioms or errors are consistent across multiple attacks. Geopolitical analysis augments technical findings, considering the broader context of international relations and strategic interests, which often illuminate why a particular target was chosen, aligning with specific nation-state agendas and capabilities; such contextual understanding can significantly narrow down potential perpetrators. Collaborative efforts across organizations and countries also enhance attribution capabilities by sharing attack data and insights, often leading to breakthroughs that would not be possible in isolation. Attribution is fraught with challenges, notably the possibility of false flags, where attackers deliberately plant evidence to mislead analysts and implicate innocent parties, a tactic that requires analysts to be exceedingly cautious and cross-verify findings through multiple independent sources. A robust attribution process involves an iterative approach, constantly refining hypotheses as new data becomes available, ensuring that conclusions are based on comprehensive and corroborative evidence. Additionally, understanding the tools and tactics used by different APT groups through active engagement in cybersecurity communities and maintaining up-to-date knowledge databases helps keep pace with evolving threats. The ultimate goal of attribution is not only to understand who is behind a given attack but also to aid in developing targeted defensive strategies and informing policy decisions, which can include diplomatic responses or proactive security measures to deter future incidents, thereby playing a crucial role in national security and cyber defense strategies. Furthermore, detailed documentation and reporting of attribution findings are essential for maintaining transparency and providing a solid foundation for potential legal actions or sanctions, which might be pursued to address or redress the consequences of hostile cyber activities by APT groups.

Chapter 4: Covert Operations and Deception Techniques

Honeypot deployment and analysis involve setting up decoy systems, applications, or data to attract cyber attackers, allowing security teams to study their behaviors and techniques without the risk of real network compromise; the primary purpose of a honeypot is to serve as an early warning system to detect, deflect, or study hacking attempts, and to gather intelligence about new malware, tactics, and potential threats by deliberately presenting vulnerabilities that are appealing to attackers. Setting up a honeypot requires careful planning to ensure it is enticing yet isolated from critical network resources; the deployment involves selecting the type of honeypot—low-interaction or high-interaction—depending on the level of engagement that the administrator wishes to simulate, with low-interaction honeypots such as Honeyd allowing for the emulation of services and operating systems without the complexity of maintaining a full system, which can be deployed using the command `honeyd -d -f honeyd.conf` where `-d` runs the daemon in debug mode and `-f` specifies the configuration file. High-interaction honeypots, on the other hand, provide real operating systems and services, which are more complex but yield more detailed data; these are typically set up using virtual machines or spare servers, isolating them to prevent potential breaches from affecting actual network operations. Monitoring tools must be configured to capture and log all interactions with the honeypot, such as attempted logins, executed commands, and network traffic, which can be achieved with tools like Snort or Wireshark, where commands like `wireshark -k -i eth0` can be used to start capturing packets on the network interface `eth0` in real-time. Analysis of honeypot data involves examining these logs to identify patterns or suspicious activities, which can inform security strategies and lead to better defensive measures against actual threats; it is also vital to keep the honeypot updated to appear vulnerable yet not too obvious to avoid detection by sophisticated attackers who might identify and avoid honeypots. Regularly updating the software and configurations of the honeypot to maintain its attractiveness and effectiveness is crucial, as is the continual analysis of the data collected to adapt to evolving threats. Data collected from honeypots can also be used to train machine learning models to detect similar attacks in real operational environments, where algorithms can learn from the attack patterns observed in the honeypot to better predict and prevent future incidents. Sharing information gathered from honeypots with the broader security community can enhance collective defense mechanisms by providing valuable insights into emerging threats and attacker methodologies. Moreover, legal considerations must be taken into account when deploying honeypots, as entrapment or privacy issues can arise if not managed properly; therefore, it's important to ensure that honeypots do not violate any laws or ethical standards, focusing strictly on defensive and educational purposes. Deploying honeypots strategically across various network segments can provide granular insight into how different types of attackers operate, whether targeting specific industries, applications, or systems, thereby enabling tailored security measures that are more effective in protecting sensitive information and critical infrastructure. In essence, honeypots serve as a proactive security tool, offering a unique and valuable perspective on the threat landscape, which, when combined with other security measures, forms a comprehensive defense strategy against cyber threats, contributing significantly to the understanding and mitigation of cyber risks in a controlled and informative manner. Deception technology implementation involves the strategic deployment of decoy systems, services, and data across a network to trick attackers into engaging with false assets, thereby revealing their presence and tactics without endangering actual network resources; this technique not only serves to mislead and detain attackers but also significantly enhances the understanding of attack methodologies, enabling organizations to fine-tune their security posture effectively. To implement deception technology, an organization first assesses its network architecture and identifies key assets that require protection, which helps in determining the placement and type of decoys that will be most effective; this may involve setting up decoy servers, databases, or even fake endpoints like workstations and IoT devices that appear fully functional but are isolated and monitored extensively. The deployment of these decoys is achieved through specialized software platforms that manage and orchestrate the decoys across the network; for instance, setting up a honeypot server using the command `docker run -d -p 80:80 --name honeypot honeypot-image` where `honeypot-image` is a Docker container designed to emulate a web server that logs and alerts on any unauthorized access attempts. The effectiveness of deception technology hinges on the realism of the decoys, which must appear as legitimate network assets to attackers; this involves not only having realistic network traffic going to and from these decoys but also ensuring that they mimic actual production environments in terms of services and data, sometimes incorporating realistic but harmless data and credentials to further entice attackers. Monitoring and alerting are critical components of deception technology, requiring the integration of deception platforms with existing security information and event management (SIEM) systems to facilitate the analysis and correlation of alert data; configuring such integrations might involve commands like `siem-tool --add-source /path/to/deception-logs --format json` to include logs from deception tools into the SIEM for comprehensive monitoring. Analysis of interactions with decoy systems provides valuable insights into attacker behavior, including the tools and tactics used, which can inform broader security strategies and threat intelligence efforts; it also allows for the identification of security gaps and the effectiveness of current defensive measures, prompting necessary adjustments. Furthermore, deception technology can automate responses to detected attacks, engaging attackers with dynamically generated responses that waste their time and resources while protecting real assets; this automation can be configured through scripting or through the deception platform's management console, specifying actions to be taken when certain types of interactions are detected. Training for IT and security teams on managing and responding to alerts generated by deception technology is essential, as is the periodic testing and validation of the deployment to ensure it remains effective and undetectable to attackers. Legal and ethical considerations must also be addressed, as the use of deception raises questions about entrapment and the handling of data collected from attackers; organizations must ensure that their use of deception technology complies with all applicable laws and standards of practice. Regular updates to deception tactics and the rotation of decoy scenarios are necessary to maintain the unpredictability and effectiveness of the technology, preventing attackers from recognizing and circumventing the decoys. Sharing the lessons learned and data gathered through deception technology with the broader cybersecurity community can also contribute to collective security efforts, enhancing the ability to preemptively address emerging cyber threats. Ultimately, deception technology represents a proactive defense mechanism that not only diverts and confuses attackers but also provides deep insights into their methods, offering a unique and powerful tool in the arsenal of cybersecurity defenses that, when implemented correctly, significantly bolsters an organization's ability to detect, analyze, and respond to cyber threats in an informed and strategic manner.

Chapter 5: Cyber Counterintelligence Tactics

Counter-deception strategies are vital in cybersecurity and intelligence operations to discern truth from manipulation by adversaries who deploy deceptive tactics, and these strategies involve a multi-layered approach focused on detection, analysis, and response to ensure that deceptive actions do not compromise security or lead to incorrect decision-making; the foundation of effective counter-deception involves thorough training of personnel to recognize potential deception, which includes understanding common tactics used by adversaries such as misinformation, honeytraps, or falsified data that can lead to wrong intelligence assessments. Building robust information verification processes is essential, where multiple sources are cross-checked to confirm the veracity of the data received, and this is particularly critical in intelligence operations where false information can lead to strategic errors; techniques like source validation, where the reliability and history of the information source are thoroughly evaluated, are implemented to ensure the integrity of intelligence. Advanced analytical tools play a crucial role in counter-deception, such as data analytics platforms that can detect anomalies or inconsistencies in data patterns that may indicate manipulation; using a command like `analyze -data /path/to/dataset --detect anomalies --output report.txt` can automate the detection of irregularities in large datasets, thereby flagging potential deceptive data for further investigation. Cybersecurity defenses must be resilient to deceptive intrusions, which involves deploying deception-detection software that can identify and alert on activities typically associated with adversary deception tactics, like unexpected access patterns or unusual communication requests within the network. Implementing redundant systems and controls also enhances the ability to withstand deceptive attacks, allowing operations to continue securely even when one line of defense is compromised. Psychological training to understand the tactics and motivations behind deception can empower analysts and decision-makers to think critically about the information they receive, questioning inconsistencies and considering alternative explanations before drawing conclusions. Regularly updating and testing security protocols to adapt to new deceptive techniques used by adversaries is crucial, as staying ahead of threat actors requires ongoing adjustments and improvements to security measures; simulations and drills can be effective in training teams to respond to deceptive scenarios, enhancing preparedness and reaction capabilities under real conditions. Collaboration among teams and with external partners increases the pooling of knowledge and resources, which helps in creating a comprehensive defense against deceptive tactics; sharing intelligence about new deception techniques or emerging threats can fortify collective security and reduce the impact of deceptive actions across multiple platforms or networks. In the realm of digital forensics, tools that can trace back the origins of an attack or the authenticity of data are invaluable; commands like `traceroute ip_address` or `dig domain_name` can help trace the path data travels from source to destination, revealing potential points of compromise or origination that might indicate deceptive routing or spoofing. Educating the wider community about the dangers and signs of deception builds a culture of security and awareness that serves as a deterrent to adversaries; this communal approach not only helps in quick identification and neutralization of threats but also strengthens societal resilience against deceptive tactics.

Legal measures and policies should be in place to penalize deceptive practices harshly, serving as a deterrent to entities considering deception as a strategy against others; this includes clear definitions of what constitutes deceptive practices in cyberspace and the imposition of consequences for those found guilty of such actions. Furthermore, investment in research to develop newer and more sophisticated counter-deception technologies and methodologies is essential to keep pace with the advancing tactics of adversaries, ensuring that defenses remain effective and relevant. Overall, counter-deception is a dynamic field that requires a blend of technical, psychological, and strategic elements, demanding a proactive and informed approach to safeguard against the manipulative and often damaging actions of adversaries, ultimately ensuring that operations and decision-making processes are based on accurate and reliable information. Defending against insider threats is an essential aspect of cybersecurity for any organization because it involves mitigating risks posed by individuals within the organization who have access to sensitive information and systems; to effectively counter these risks, a multifaceted approach is required that incorporates both technical solutions and human-centric strategies, starting with the implementation of strict access controls which limit users' access to only the information necessary for their roles, thereby reducing the potential for unauthorized data access or malicious activities, this principle, known as the least privilege, can be enforced through Active Directory group policies or similar tools where administrators can set permissions based on job roles using commands like `Set-ADGroup -Identity "GroupName" -Replace @{grouptype='Security'; groupscope='Global'}`, furthermore, user activity monitoring is another critical layer of defense, involving the tracking and logging of user actions to identify unusual or unauthorized activities that could indicate a threat, for this, tools such as SIEM (Security Information and Event Management) systems can be employed which aggregate and analyze logs from various sources across the network, enabling real-time detection of potential threats through alerts and automated responses configured using commands like `New-SysmonConfig -RuleName "Unauthorized Access" -EventType "CreateProcess" -Action "Alert"`.

Additionally, organizations should implement comprehensive auditing and reporting practices that ensure all access and activity are transparent and traceable, this can be achieved by setting up audit policies that log key events and changes, commands like `auditpol /set /subcategory:"File System" /success:enable /failure:enable` are used to configure auditing rules on Windows servers, allowing security teams to keep a close watch on file access and modifications which could be indicative of insider threats, alongside these technical measures, robust security policies and regular training sessions for employees play a crucial role in reinforcing the importance of security and educating staff on the potential indicators of insider threats as well as the proper protocols to follow when they suspect a security breach, these policies should be clear, concise, and easily accessible to all employees, ensuring they understand the consequences of violating company security protocols and the importance of reporting suspicious behavior.

On top of policies and training, behavioral analysis is becoming an increasingly important tool in the detection of insider threats, by using machine learning algorithms and statistical models, systems can analyze patterns of user behavior to detect anomalies that deviate from normal activities, these systems can be configured using tools like `Import-Module PSBehave; New-BehaviorRule -Name "Unusual After-Hours Access" -Condition "Time -gt '18:00' - and Time -lt '06:00'"`, which helps in identifying actions performed outside of normal working hours, an indicator of potential insider threat activities, such techniques are essential for early detection and response, which can significantly mitigate the impact of insider threats.

In addition to setting up defenses, it is also vital for organizations to have a response plan in place to address insider threats when they are detected; this plan should outline specific steps to be taken during and after an incident, including how to contain the threat, communicate with stakeholders, and how to recover from the breach, using tools like incident response platforms that can orchestrate and automate responses with commands like `Invoke-IRWorkflow -Name "Insider Threat Containment"`, organizations can quickly and effectively respond to incidents without losing critical time during a crisis, ensuring that they can minimize damage and begin the process of recovery and analysis to prevent future breaches.

Moreover, continuous improvement of security practices through regular audits, updates to security policies, and incorporation of new technologies is crucial to staying ahead of potential insider threats, as attackers continually evolve their strategies and techniques, so too must the defenses that protect against them, this means regularly updating systems, applying security patches, and revising access controls and monitoring strategies to close any gaps that might be exploited by malicious insiders, it is a relentless task that requires ongoing commitment and vigilance from every part of the organization.

Lastly, fostering a culture of security within the organization is perhaps the most fundamental aspect of defending against insider threats, when employees feel a sense of responsibility and ownership over their roles in the security posture of the organization, they are more likely to adhere to policies and report suspicious activities, creating a collaborative environment where security is seen as a collective effort can greatly enhance the effectiveness of the technical and procedural safeguards in place, thereby strengthening the overall security framework and reducing the likelihood of insider threats becoming a detrimental issue within the organization.

Chapter 6: Insider Threat Detection and Mitigation

Behavioral analytics for insider threat detection is a sophisticated approach that leverages data analysis techniques to identify unusual patterns of behavior that might indicate malicious or unintentional insider threats; this technique is crucial as it provides an additional layer of security that complements traditional security measures by focusing on the subtler, psychological aspects of security which are often overlooked, for instance, an organization might use a behavioral analytics tool that collects and analyzes log data from various systems and applications to create a baseline of normal user activity, and any deviations from this baseline could trigger alerts for further investigation, these systems can be set up using commands like `Import-Module PSBehave; New-BehaviorRule -Name "Unusual After-Hours Access" -Condition "Time -gt '18:00' -and Time -lt '06:00'"`, which helps in identifying actions performed outside of normal working hours, an indicator of potential insider threat activities.

By employing machine learning algorithms, these tools analyze vast amounts of data to detect anomalies that are too subtle for traditional security measures to catch, for example, if an employee suddenly starts accessing files at unusual times or downloading large amounts of data, the behavioral analytics system can flag these actions as suspicious based on the deviation from their usual behavior patterns, configuring these alerts can be achieved by setting up parameters in the behavioral analytics software, such as `Set-BAParameter -ProfileName "FinanceTeam" -AnomalyDetection On -Threshold 75`, which activates anomaly detection for the finance team profiles and sets a sensitivity threshold.

Furthermore, behavioral analytics can also identify trends that might indicate a more widespread issue within the organization, such as multiple employees accessing sensitive data they normally do not need to access, these patterns can be identified using aggregation and correlation functions within the analytics platform, which can be configured to generate reports and alerts through commands like `New-CorrelationAlert -Name "Multiple Sensitive File Access" -Pattern "MultipleAccess" -Action "NotifySecurityTeam"`, enabling security teams to take proactive steps to investigate and mitigate potential threats before they escalate into serious breaches.

Moreover, the integration of behavioral analytics into the existing security infrastructure is typically achieved through the use of APIs that allow disparate systems to communicate and share data, commands like `Connect-BAPI -Uri "https://api.example.com" -Credential $(Get-Credential)` are used to establish connections to these APIs, allowing behavioral analytics tools to pull data from various sources such as network traffic logs, email servers, and database transactions to create a comprehensive view of user behavior across the organization.

In addition to automated monitoring and detection, behavioral analytics tools often include capabilities for forensic analysis, allowing security analysts to dig deeper into suspicious activities and understand the context around them, this might involve using commands like `Get-BALog -UserID "JohnDoe" -Date "2023-06-01" -Verbose` to retrieve detailed logs related to a specific user's activities on a given date, providing insights that can help determine whether an incident is a false positive or a genuine threat.

The effective use of behavioral analytics also depends on the continuous tuning and calibration of the system, as user behavior can change over time due to new job responsibilities, shifts in work patterns, or changes in technology, commands such as `Update-BABaseline -ProfileID "UserProfile01" -RecalculateBasedOnLast '30Days'` can be used to update the baseline model of normal behavior for a user profile based on the most recent 30 days of activity, ensuring that the system remains accurate and reduces false positives.

To further enhance the effectiveness of behavioral analytics, many organizations combine it with other security practices such as user education and awareness programs, which help employees understand the types of behaviors that are flagged by these systems and the importance of adhering to company policies, thereby reducing the likelihood of unintentional insider threats and helping to foster a culture of security awareness throughout the organization.

Ultimately, behavioral analytics for insider threat detection is a powerful tool that, when effectively integrated and managed, can significantly enhance an organization's ability to detect and respond to insider threats, by providing a deep understanding of user behavior and identifying potential risks before they result in data breaches or other security incidents, organizations can maintain a strong security posture and protect their critical assets from both malicious insiders and unintentional threats. Insider threat incident response strategies are essential for organizations to effectively manage and mitigate risks associated with malicious or unintentional actions from employees or contractors who have legitimate access to the organization's systems and data; the first step in crafting these strategies involves the development of a detailed incident response plan that specifically addresses potential insider threats, this plan should outline clear procedures and roles for detecting, analyzing, containing, eradicating, and recovering from insider incidents, and it is crucial that the plan includes both technical and non-technical measures, such as the legal and HR responses necessary when dealing with employees implicated in an incident, furthermore, deploying an insider threat detection system involves configuring tools and processes that can alert the security team to suspicious activities, for instance, setting up a SIEM system to monitor for unusual access patterns or large data transfers typically involves commands like `New-SIEMRule -Name "Unauthorized Access Alert" -Pattern "MultipleFailedLogins | LargeUploads" -Action "NotifySecurityTeam"`, which triggers an alert when it detects multiple failed login attempts or large data uploads outside of normal operational hours.

Once a potential insider threat is detected, the incident response team must act swiftly to verify and assess the severity of the incident, using tools such as advanced forensic analysis software that can track user activities and changes to system configurations or data, for example, forensic commands such as `Get-ForensicTimeline -ComputerID "12345" -FromDate "2023-01-01" -ToDate "2023-01-02"` can be utilized to create a detailed timeline of all activities performed by the suspected insider within a specified period, this timeline aids in understanding the extent of the incident and determining whether it was a deliberate, malicious act or a simple error, next, containment strategies are crucial to prevent further damage and involve restricting the suspected insider's access to sensitive information while maintaining necessary access to ensure business continuity, this might involve modifying access controls using commands like `Set-UserAccess -UserID "JohnDoe" -AccessLevel "Restricted" -ApplyTo "SensitiveFiles"`, which limits access to sensitive files while the investigation is ongoing.

Following containment, eradication involves removing any unauthorized changes made by the insider, such as unauthorized software installations or data modifications, commands like `Remove-UnauthorizedSoftware -SoftwareName "UnknownApp" -ComputerID "67890"` can be used to uninstall any unauthorized software found during the investigation, recovery processes then restore systems and data to their state before the incident, ensuring that all systems are clean and fully functional, this often involves restoring data from backups and verifying that no traces of the threat remain, commands such as `Restore-File -FromBackup "BackupID123" -ToFileLocation "/SensitiveData" -Date "2023-01-01"` can be employed to restore files from a backup made prior to the incident.

Additionally, after an incident has been resolved, it is imperative to conduct a thorough review of how it was handled to identify any gaps in the response process and to improve future responses, this post-incident analysis should include a detailed review of the effectiveness of the response, lessons learned, and recommendations for preventing similar incidents in the future, organizations might use commands like `Generate-IncidentReport -IncidentID "45678" -OutputFormat "PDF"` to generate a detailed report of the incident, which can then be analyzed to improve the incident response plan.

Furthermore, insider threat incident response is not just about managing the incidents themselves but also about building a robust deterrence strategy that includes policies, procedures, and controls designed to prevent insider incidents before they occur, this includes conducting regular security training and awareness programs that educate employees about the types of behaviors that are monitored and the consequences of violating company policies, additionally, it involves ongoing assessments of user behaviors and access patterns, which can be enhanced by automated tools that continuously analyze and flag unusual activities, ensuring that potential threats are identified and addressed promptly.

In summary, effective insider threat incident response requires a well-orchestrated approach combining policy, technology, and procedures to detect, respond to, and recover from incidents, while also educating employees and continuously improving security practices to mitigate the risk of future incidents, this multi-layered approach ensures that organizations can protect their critical assets from the potentially devastating effects of insider threats.

Chapter 7: Advanced Digital Forensic Techniques

Data carving and file fragment recovery are advanced forensic techniques used to retrieve data from digital storage media, especially helpful when dealing with files that are not referenced in the file system metadata, typically as a result of deletion or damage to the file system; these techniques are particularly crucial in computer forensics and data recovery operations where traditional methods of file retrieval fail because data carving does not rely on standard file system structures but instead examines the raw binary data on the disk, searching for file signatures and using them to reconstruct files, a common scenario where data carving is applied includes recovering remnants of deleted files from unallocated disk space where file system metadata no longer references the file content, and to perform data carving, tools like `foremost` can be used, which can be initiated with a command such as `foremost -i /dev/sda -o /recovery/output -t jpg,pdf` to recover jpg and pdf files from a drive.

In addition to general data recovery, file fragment recovery involves piecing together bits of data that belong to a damaged or partially overwritten file, a process that is particularly challenging but crucial for extracting usable information from corrupted files, typically, the process begins with an analysis of the storage medium to identify fragments of files using techniques such as header/footer matching, where the recovery tool scans for known file headers and footers, then attempts to reconstruct the content between these markers, this can be done using `scalpel`, a file carving tool configured by a scalpel configuration file where you specify headers and footers of file types you want to recover, with a command like `scalpel /dev/sda -o /recovery/output -c /etc/scalpel/scalpel.conf`, which directs the tool to carve files from the disk `/dev/sda` into the output directory based on rules defined in the `scalpel.conf` configuration file.

Additionally, more sophisticated data carving techniques such as file carving based on content analysis are employed when header/footer techniques are insufficient; this involves analyzing the content of file fragments to identify patterns or metadata that can suggest the file type or part of the file structure, sometimes involving the use of machine learning algorithms to improve the accuracy of predictions about where a file starts and ends in a stream of binary data, tools like `PhotoRec` are often used in these scenarios, which can be executed with commands like `photorec /d /recovery/output /dev/sda` to recover files based on content patterns from the disk.

Furthermore, the effectiveness of data carving can be enhanced by combining it with other forensic techniques such as timeline analysis, which helps to establish when the file fragments were created or last modified, often crucial in legal contexts where the timing of data creation, modification, or deletion may be disputed; timeline analysis can be performed using tools like `fls` from The Sleuth Kit, where you can generate a timeline with `fls -m / -r /dev/sda | mactime -b - > /recovery/timeline.txt`, creating a comprehensive timeline of all file system actions recorded on the device.

It is also important to handle the recovered data with care to maintain its integrity for legal proceedings; forensic analysts typically use write blockers when accessing original media to prevent any modification to the data, and all recovery operations are conducted on images of the original data rather than the original media itself to preserve the evidence in its original state, a standard practice in the field involves creating a forensic image of the drive using a command like `dd if=/dev/sda of=/forensic/image.dd bs=4M` to create a bit-for-bit copy of the drive which can then be analyzed without risk of data alteration.

Moreover, as file systems and storage technologies evolve, data recovery techniques must also adapt to these changes, including the development of new carving techniques for emerging file types and the improvement of algorithms to deal with the increasing size and complexity of storage media; ongoing research and development in this area are essential to keep up with the advancements in digital technology and to improve the success rates of data recovery efforts.

In practice, data carving and file fragment recovery require a deep understanding of file structures, storage media, and forensic techniques, as well as patience and attention to detail, since the process can be time-consuming and complex, often involving the examination of large volumes of data to find the pieces needed to reconstruct a file, the work is meticulous and often requires trial and error to achieve successful outcomes, underscoring the importance of expertise and specialized tools in the field of digital forensics. Timeline analysis in digital investigations is a forensic technique used to create a comprehensive chronological sequence of events by examining timestamps and other time-related data on digital devices, which can help investigators understand the sequence in which events occurred, potentially pinpointing when illegal or unauthorized activities took place; this method is vital in piecing together digital evidence, providing a clearer picture of the actions and behaviors of individuals involved in the investigation, to perform timeline analysis, forensic experts utilize a variety of tools and software to extract time-related data from system logs, file metadata, and other sources, for example, using `The Sleuth Kit` (TSK), which includes tools like `fls` to list file and directory names in a file system, combined with `mactime` that creates a timeline of file modifications, accesses, changes, and creations from data generated by `fls`, and this can be executed with commands like `fls -m / -r /dev/sda | mactime -d > timeline.txt`, which outputs a detailed timeline to a text file for further analysis.

Beyond just listing events, advanced timeline analysis often involves integrating data from multiple sources and devices to build a more comprehensive timeline, incorporating data from network logs, email servers, and other electronic records, which can be correlated using specialized software like `Log2Timeline`, a tool that extracts timestamps from various files found on a typical computer system and aggregates them into a super timeline that can be easily searched and analyzed, one can run `log2timeline.py /output/parsed_timeline.plaso /input/image.dd` to process an image file and produce a plaso file, which then can be analyzed with `psort.py -z UTC /output/parsed_timeline.plaso > /output/final_timeline.csv`, making it possible to sort and filter the timeline based on different criteria, such as date, type of event, or involved user.

The meticulous process of timeline analysis also entails examining anomalies in the data, like timestamps that appear manipulated or out of sequence, which can indicate tampering or use of anti-forensic techniques; investigators must be vigilant and consider the context of each artifact within the timeline, often requiring cross-referencing with physical evidence or other digital data to confirm the reliability of timestamp data, this detailed scrutiny might reveal patterns such as the deletion of files immediately following unauthorized access or suspicious activities at unusual hours, providing critical insights into the behavior of potential suspects.

Furthermore, in the context of corporate investigations, timeline analysis can reveal the exfiltration of data, as it often involves large file transfers or emailing of sensitive data just before an employee leaves a company or immediately following notification of termination, detailed timelines help human resources and IT security departments understand and act upon these incidents more effectively, ensuring that appropriate measures can be taken to secure enterprise data and possibly recover stolen information.

Moreover, timeline analysis is not only about identifying the past actions but also about helping to prevent future incidents by establishing patterns of behavior that may indicate lapses in security or vulnerabilities within system configurations, ongoing monitoring and analysis can alert administrators to unauthorized changes in real-time, allowing quicker responses to potential security breaches, which can be crucial for organizations facing advanced persistent threats where attackers have sustained access to a network over extended periods.

In legal contexts, the ability to provide a detailed and accurate timeline based on forensic analysis can be pivotal in court, serving as evidence to support claims about when and how digital activities occurred, lawyers and experts often rely on timelines to make or break cases involving data theft, fraud, cyberstalking, or even more severe crimes like terrorism or child exploitation, the credibility and clarity of digital evidence are often enhanced by a well-documented timeline that can be easily understood by judges and juries, who may not be familiar with the technical aspects of digital forensics.

Given the increasing complexity of digital environments and the volume of data typically involved in investigations, automation in timeline analysis is becoming more prevalent, using scripts and batch processing to handle large datasets and reduce the manual workload on forensic analysts, this includes the use of command-line tools that can automate the extraction and processing of time-related data from a variety of sources, further enhancing the efficiency and accuracy of investigations.

In essence, timeline analysis in digital investigations provides a fundamental framework for understanding and documenting the sequence of events in a digital space, enabling forensic experts, corporate security officers, and law enforcement agencies to uncover the truth in complex cases involving digital media, the deployment of sophisticated forensic tools and techniques in timeline analysis not only streamlines the investigative process but also deepens the understanding of digital events, thereby playing a critical role in both solving cases and enhancing cybersecurity measures.

Chapter 8: Cryptanalysis and Code-breaking Methods

Cryptographic protocol analysis is a crucial practice in the field of cybersecurity, focusing on the examination and validation of protocols designed to secure communications by encrypting messages and authenticating user identities, where the primary goal is to identify potential vulnerabilities that could be exploited to compromise the security of data transmissions; this analysis involves a detailed review of how cryptographic protocols are implemented, including the algorithms used, the key management techniques, and the protocol execution environment, ensuring that the cryptographic measures comply with established security standards and are robust against various types of cyber threats, experts in this field use a variety of tools and techniques to dissect protocols, including formal verification methods and automated tools that can model protocol behaviors and check for flaws like replay attacks, race conditions, or improper error handling.

One common method in cryptographic protocol analysis is to perform a static analysis of the protocol implementation code, using tools like Cryptol, which provides a specialized language designed for specifying cryptographic algorithms in a way that is amenable to formal verification, you might use a command like `cryptol verify protocolSpec.cry` to check that the protocol specification adheres to its intended security properties, this can uncover discrepancies between the protocol's design and its actual implementation which could lead to vulnerabilities if left unaddressed; additionally, dynamic analysis might involve running the protocol in a controlled environment where its operations can be monitored and analyzed to detect runtime vulnerabilities that static analysis might miss, this often includes setting up test cases that simulate attacks or unexpected conditions to see how the protocol responds, using network simulation tools like Wireshark or more specialized software like Scapy with a command like `scapy run -c tls_test_case.py` to execute a series of custom test scripts designed to probe the resilience of TLS implementations.

Another critical aspect of cryptographic protocol analysis is the analysis of cryptographic keys and their management because the security of any cryptographic system relies heavily on the strength and secrecy of its keys, therefore, part of the protocol analysis involves reviewing how keys are generated, distributed, stored, and destroyed, ensuring that they cannot easily be compromised or recovered by unauthorized entities, tools like OpenSSL can be used to examine the properties of cryptographic keys with commands such as `openssl rsa -in private.key -check` to verify the integrity and security of RSA private keys.

In addition to these technical analyses, cryptographic protocol analysis also considers the practical aspects of protocol deployment in real-world environments, which includes assessing the performance impact of cryptographic operations on system resources and the usability of the protocol, which can affect how reliably and effectively the protocol will be used, for instance, a protocol that significantly slows down system performance or complicates user interactions might lead to insecure configurations or workarounds that undermine the protocol's security objectives.

Moreover, with the evolution of quantum computing, cryptographic protocol analysis is increasingly focusing on quantum-resistant protocols, which are designed to be secure against the potential future threat posed by quantum computers that could break many of the cryptographic systems currently in use; this involves researching and analyzing new types of cryptographic algorithms such as lattice-based, hash-based, or multivariate quadratic equations which are believed to be resistant to quantum attacks, using tools like the Microsoft Quantum Development Kit to simulate how these algorithms perform under quantum conditions with a command line invocation like `qdk simulate algorithm.qs` can provide insights into the feasibility and security of these quantum-resistant algorithms.

Cryptographic protocol analysis also plays a crucial role in regulatory compliance, as many industries have strict requirements for data protection that include the use of approved cryptographic protocols, analysts must ensure that protocols not only meet current security standards but are also aligned with legal and regulatory frameworks, this might involve conducting compliance audits using guidelines from standards bodies like NIST or ISO, which stipulate which cryptographic methods are acceptable for protecting sensitive data.

The ultimate aim of cryptographic protocol analysis is to ensure that communication and data exchange over digital networks are secure from interception, manipulation, and unauthorized access, by rigorously testing and verifying the security of cryptographic protocols, organizations can safeguard their information assets against the evolving landscape of cyber threats, while also ensuring the trust and confidence of their users and partners in the integrity and confidentiality of their communications, this ongoing process requires continuous attention as new vulnerabilities are discovered and new security technologies emerge. Brute force and dictionary attack techniques are common methods used in cybersecurity to crack passwords and gain unauthorized access to systems, with brute force attacks involving the systematic checking of all possible passwords until the correct one is found, a method that, while straightforward, requires significant computational power and time, especially as the complexity of the password increases, these attacks can be executed using tools such as `John the Ripper` or `hashcat`, for example, executing a brute force attack with hashcat might involve a command like `hashcat -a 3 -m 0 hash.txt ?a?a?a?a?a?a`, where `-a 3` designates brute force mode, `-m 0` specifies the hash type, and `?a?a?a?a?a?a` defines a six-character password using all available characters.

In contrast, dictionary attacks are more refined, utilizing a file containing words, phrases, or common passwords instead of random combinations, operating under the assumption that many users choose passwords that are words or easy-to-remember combinations that might already exist in a pre-compiled list, reducing the time needed to crack a password significantly; to carry out a dictionary attack using `John the Ripper`, you might use a command like `john --wordlist=passwords.txt hash.txt`, where `passwords.txt` is a file containing potential passwords and `hash.txt` contains the password hashes to be tested.

Both techniques have evolved with the introduction of hybrid attacks, which combine the thoroughness of brute force attacks with the efficiency of dictionary attacks, typically by appending or prepending numbers and symbols to dictionary words to crack passwords that are not simple words but also not entirely random, using a command such as `hashcat -a 6 hash.txt passwords.txt ?d?d`, which appends two digits to each word in `passwords.txt` for a hybrid dictionary attack, thereby increasing the likelihood of matching a password that includes common numerical additions.

Moreover, the effectiveness of these attacks can often be enhanced by the use of rules that modify the dictionary words according to common user habits, such as replacing letters with numbers, capitalizing letters, or reversing the order of characters, for instance, in `hashcat`, you can specify rule-based attacks using `-r` followed by the rule file, with a command like `hashcat -a 0 -m 100 -r rules/best64.rule hash.txt passwords.txt`, where `rules/b

est64.rule` is a file containing specific rules that adjust the dictionary words in sophisticated ways, addressing common modifications users might make to their passwords.

The deployment of these attacks also considers the type of hash function used to secure passwords, as different hash algorithms offer varying levels of security and resistance to cracking efforts; for example, cracking a password hashed with a robust algorithm like bcrypt requires much more computational time and power compared to older or less secure hashing mechanisms like MD5 or SHA1, a factor that is critical in choosing the attack method and tool, as some tools specialize in certain types of hashes and may offer optimized performance for them.

As defense mechanisms against brute force and dictionary attacks have strengthened, including the implementation of account lockout policies and the requirement for more complex password criteria, attackers have responded by refining their techniques and utilizing more powerful hardware or botnets to distribute the computational load, enabling faster cracking of even complex passwords over multiple machines; furthermore, the advent of GPUs and specialized hardware like FPGA boards has dramatically increased the feasibility and speed of performing high-rate password guessing attacks, using commands in `hashcat` that enable GPU-based cracking such as `hashcat -m 1700 -a 0 -o cracked.txt --opencl-device-types 1,2,3 hash.txt passwords.txt` to utilize all available OpenCL device types in the system.

Additionally, attackers often enhance their dictionary attack databases with leaked passwords from data breaches, creating a feedback loop where each new large-scale breach potentially provides a richer set of common passwords and patterns for future attacks, this practice underscores the importance of not only securing password storage through hashing and salting but also educating users about the risks of reusing passwords across multiple sites and services.

Preventing these attacks not only involves technical measures such as enforcing strong password policies, implementing multi-factor authentication, and using CAPTCHAs to thwart automated login attempts but also requires ongoing vigilance in monitoring access logs for unusual activity that might indicate an attempt to breach systems using brute force or dictionary methods; these logs can be monitored using automated tools that trigger alerts based on anomalous behavior, with commands like `grep 'Failed password' /var/log/auth.log | awk '{print $11}' | sort | uniq -c | sort -nr` to analyze Unix system logs for repeated failed password attempts from the same IP address, which might suggest a brute force attack in progress.

Ultimately, the continuous evolution of password cracking techniques demands equally dynamic and robust security practices from organizations and individuals alike, requiring a multi-layered security approach that includes both proactive measures to make cracking excessively time-consuming or computationally expensive and reactive monitoring mechanisms to quickly detect and respond to potential breaches, ensuring that security systems and policies are regularly reviewed and updated in response to the ever-changing landscape of threats and vulnerabilities in the digital world.

Chapter 9: Cyber Espionage and Nation-State Attacks

Attribution of nation-state sponsored attacks in cybersecurity is an incredibly complex and sensitive endeavor, involving the identification of the perpetrators behind cyber attacks that are believed to be backed or directed by national governments, this task is fraught with challenges due to the sophisticated tactics employed by attackers to mask their identities and origins, as well as the geopolitical implications that can arise from attributing cyber attacks to specific countries; in the process of attribution, cybersecurity experts and intelligence agencies rely heavily on a mix of technical forensics, human intelligence, and geopolitical analysis to piece together the evidence that could point to a nation-state actor, one of the first steps in this process involves the collection and analysis of digital forensic data from the compromised systems, where experts look for indicators of compromise (IoCs) that might include specific malware signatures, IP addresses, and tactics, techniques, and procedures (TTPs) associated with known nation-state actors, using tools like `YARA` to create and apply rules that help in identifying and classifying malware samples based on patterns and binaries found in the attack data, a command like `yara -r myrules.yar /suspect/files` helps scan directories for patterns defined in the YARA rules, which might link the attack to previously known nation-state tools or campaigns.

Further analysis might involve examining network traffic logs to trace back the origins of the attack, potentially using tools like `Wireshark` or `tcpdump` to capture and analyze packets, commands like `tcpdump -i eth0 -nn -s0 -w output.pcap` can be used to capture all packets on the `eth0` interface, saving them to a file for later examination, which could reveal command and control (C2) servers and other network indicators linked to known nation-state groups; alongside technical evidence, analysts also consider the context of the attack, including its timing, target, and potential motives, which might align with the strategic interests or ongoing geopolitical activities of certain countries, this contextual analysis helps in distinguishing between nation-state actors and other types of cybercriminals who typically lack a political motive.

Adding to the complexity, nation-state attackers often use proxy groups or compromised third-party systems to carry out their attacks, which further obscures their identity and makes direct attribution more challenging; to address this, attribution efforts may involve collaboration with international cybersecurity organizations and other governments to share intelligence and corroborate findings, such collaboration might be facilitated through platforms like `MISP` (Malware Information Sharing Platform), where commands like `misp-search -g malware -t "nation-state"` can be used to search shared threat intelligence databases for information related to malware used in suspected nation-state attacks.

Moreover, attribution is not merely a technical challenge but also a political one, as incorrectly attributing a cyber attack to a nation-state can have serious diplomatic consequences, hence, governments and organizations often proceed with caution, sometimes choosing to withhold attribution publicly while using the information for internal or diplomatic actions; this delicate balance between transparency, accountability, and geopolitical strategy underscores the complexity of attributing nation-state sponsored attacks, making it one of the most nuanced aspects of cybersecurity.

In some cases, the attribution can be supported by historical patterns where specific nation-states have been observed conducting similar types of attacks against similar targets, such as critical infrastructure systems or political organizations, the consistency of these patterns over time can help analysts and policymakers draw connections between new attacks and past activities, reinforcing the credibility of the attribution despite the inherent challenges; additionally, advancements in cybersecurity technology and techniques continue to improve the capabilities for attribution, including the development of artificial intelligence models that can analyze vast amounts of data more quickly and accurately than human analysts, potentially recognizing subtle patterns that link different cyber campaigns to the same perpetrators.

Despite these advancements, the field of cybersecurity recognizes the limits of attribution; it is often described as more of an art than a science, requiring not just technical expertise but also strategic thinking and careful judgment, making it a pivotal aspect of national security strategies in the digital age, where cyber warfare plays an increasingly prominent role in global geopolitics, necessitating ongoing investment in cybersecurity defenses, international cooperation, and the development of legal and ethical frameworks for cyber warfare and espionage that help manage the complexities associated with attributing and responding to nation-state sponsored attacks. Case studies of cyber espionage campaigns reveal the intricate and stealthy nature of these operations, often orchestrated by nation-states or state-sponsored entities aiming to gather intelligence, influence foreign policy, or gain economic advantages; one notable example is the Stuxnet virus, discovered in 2010, which specifically targeted Iranian nuclear facilities and is believed to have been developed by the United States and Israel, this sophisticated piece of malware exploited multiple zero-day vulnerabilities and spread through infected USB drives, subtly altering the speed of centrifuges in the facilities to damage them without detection, analysis of Stuxnet required advanced forensic techniques, with security experts using tools like `IDA Pro` to disassemble the binary and scrutinize the code, finding evidence of its origins and methods, a command such as `ida -B stuxnet_binary.exe` would initiate a batch disassembly of the executable, providing valuable insights into its construction and operation.

Another significant case is the 2015 breach of the United States Office of Personnel Management (OPM), attributed to Chinese state-sponsored hackers; this breach involved the exfiltration of sensitive personal data of approximately 22 million current and former federal employees, the attackers initially gained access through a third-party contractor's credentials, then escalated privileges to install a backdoor and establish a persistent presence on the network, using tools likely similar to `Mimikatz` to harvest credentials, a typical command executed might be `mimikatz "privilege::debug" "sekurlsa::logonpasswords"`, which extracts passwords and other authentication tokens from memory, the OPM breach highlighted the need for stringent security measures including multi-factor authentication and rigorous monitoring of third-party vendors.

In 2014, the Dragonfly campaign targeted energy grid operators, major electricity generation firms, and petroleum pipeline operators, primarily in the United States and Europe; the attackers, believed to be Russian, used spear-phishing and water-holing tactics to compromise networks and potentially disrupt energy supplies, forensic analysis in such a scenario might involve examining web server logs for indicators of the water-holing attack, employing commands like `grep "suspicious_parameter" /var/log/apache2/access.log` to identify potentially malicious traffic, this campaign underscored the importance of defending critical infrastructure against cyber threats by enforcing network segmentation, robust authentication practices, and continuous monitoring for anomalous activities.

Further, the 2017 WannaCry ransomware attack, though widely regarded as a financially motivated cybercrime, had significant implications for national security given its rapid global spread and disruptive impact on the United Kingdom's National Health Service and other critical services worldwide; WannaCry utilized the EternalBlue exploit, which leveraged a vulnerability in Microsoft Windows SMB protocol, analysts at security firms and national cybersecurity agencies used network scanning tools like `Nmap` to assess the extent of the vulnerability within their networks, running commands like `nmap -p 445 --script smb-vuln-ms17-010 -oN vulnerable_hosts.txt` to identify hosts vulnerable to the EternalBlue exploit, this case illustrated the potential for cyber tools developed as espionage instruments to be repurposed by criminal groups, highlighting the dual-use nature of cyber exploits and the need for careful handling of cyber weapons.

These case studies demonstrate not only the diverse tactics employed in cyber espionage but also the broad spectrum of targets and motives behind these campaigns, ranging from political and military espionage to economic and industrial sabotage, they emphasize the critical role of advanced cybersecurity measures, threat intelligence sharing, and international cooperation in preventing and responding to such threats, ensuring that organizations and governments remain vigilant and prepared against the evolving landscape of cyber threats, while also fostering discussions on cyber norms and regulations to address the challenges posed by state-sponsored cyber activities and their implications for global security and stability.

Chapter 10: Strategic Incident Response Planning

Developing incident response playbooks is an essential process for organizations aiming to prepare and streamline their approach to handling cybersecurity incidents efficiently; these playbooks provide detailed, step-by-step instructions that guide the incident response team through the phases of identifying, investigating, containing, eradicating, and recovering from security breaches, along with documenting and reviewing the incident to improve future responses, the foundation of a strong incident response playbook begins with a clear understanding of the organization's IT infrastructure, key assets, and potential threats, which helps in crafting specific response strategies tailored to different types of incidents such as data breaches, ransomware attacks, or DDoS attacks, from there, the playbook should outline roles and responsibilities clearly, specifying who is in charge of each step in the incident response process, this includes designating a team leader, communications officer, and other key roles such as forensic analysts, legal advisors, and human resources representatives depending on the nature of the incident.

The creation of these playbooks often involves the collaboration of various stakeholders within the organization, including IT, security, legal, and communications departments, ensuring that all perspectives are considered and that the response actions comply with legal and regulatory requirements; for example, if an organization faces a data breach involving sensitive customer information, the playbook should include specific steps for complying with data protection regulations such as GDPR or HIPAA, which might involve commands to isolate affected systems and secure logs for analysis, such as `iptables -A INPUT -s 192.168.0.12 -j DROP` to block incoming traffic from a suspicious IP address, or `rsync -avz /var/log/ /backup/logs/` to securely backup current log files for further investigation.

Additionally, incident response playbooks should be regularly updated to reflect the changing cyber threat landscape and lessons learned from past incidents, this could involve revising contact lists, updating software tools, or incorporating new regulatory requirements into the response procedures, regular training sessions and drills should also be conducted to ensure that the incident response team is familiar with the playbook and can execute its procedures under pressure, during these drills, simulated attacks are carried out and the response is monitored to identify any weaknesses in the playbook or in the team's execution of the response, which is critical for ensuring that the team can respond effectively to a real incident.

To enhance the functionality of a playbook, automation can be incorporated to handle routine tasks such as alerting, initial data collection, and basic containment measures, for instance, using a security orchestration, automation, and response (SOAR) platform, commands like `soar-tool trigger --playbook "phishing_response.yml" --alert-id 12345` can automatically initiate a predefined playbook for responding to phishing incidents, saving valuable time and allowing human responders to focus on more complex tasks like analysis and decision-making.

In the playbook, detailed procedures for communication should be outlined, both internally to the organization and externally to customers, regulators, and possibly the media, ensuring that all communications are clear, accurate, and delivered in a timely manner to manage the situation effectively and maintain trust; this might include predefined templates for breach notifications, press releases, and customer communications that can be quickly adapted to the specifics of an incident.

Furthermore, the playbook should include guidelines for the use of forensic tools and techniques to preserve evidence in a manner that is admissible in court if necessary; this includes using write-blockers when accessing affected drives and ensuring that all forensic analysis is performed on copies of the data rather than the original evidence, commands such as `dd if=/dev/sda of=/mnt/backup/sda.img conv=noerror,sync bs=64K` can be used to create a bit-by-bit image of a compromised drive for analysis without altering the original evidence.

By creating comprehensive and actionable incident response playbooks, organizations can significantly enhance their preparedness for cybersecurity incidents, reducing the impact on operations and reputation by ensuring a coordinated and effective response, such playbooks serve not only as a guide during an incident but also as a tool for ongoing security management and improvement, making them a vital component of any organization's cybersecurity strategy. Incident response tabletop exercises are invaluable tools for organizations aiming to enhance their preparedness against cyber threats and other emergencies. These simulated scenarios simulate real-life incidents, allowing teams to practice their response strategies in a controlled environment. The exercises typically involve key stakeholders from various departments, including IT, security, legal, and communications, who collaborate to assess and mitigate the simulated incident. Through these exercises, teams can identify weaknesses in their incident response plans, refine communication protocols, and improve coordination among different departments.

One of the primary objectives of conducting tabletop exercises is to test the organization's incident response plan (IRP) under realistic conditions without actual disruption to operations. This proactive approach helps teams familiarize themselves with their roles and responsibilities during a crisis, ensuring a more efficient and coordinated response when a real incident occurs. Participants are often presented with a scenario relevant to their industry, such as a data breach, malware infection, or a ransomware attack, and are tasked with making decisions and taking actions as they would in a real-world situation.

During these exercises, facilitators play a crucial role in guiding discussions, introducing new developments in the scenario, and challenging participants to think critically about their responses. This dynamic environment encourages active participation and prompts teams to consider different aspects of incident handling, including technical remediation, legal implications, public relations strategies, and regulatory compliance. By simulating the pressures and uncertainties of a crisis, tabletop exercises help organizations build resilience and improve their overall incident response capabilities.

To ensure the effectiveness of tabletop exercises, it is essential to define clear objectives and realistic scenarios that align with the organization's risk profile and threat landscape. Tailoring scenarios to specific cybersecurity threats or regulatory requirements helps participants understand the potential impact of different incidents on business operations and customer trust. For example, organizations in highly regulated industries may focus on scenarios related to data privacy breaches or compliance violations to test their ability to respond within legal constraints.

Moreover, tabletop exercises provide an opportunity to evaluate the effectiveness of technical controls and incident detection mechanisms. Participants may discuss the deployment of security monitoring tools, intrusion detection systems, and endpoint protection solutions to identify indicators of compromise and contain the simulated incident. This hands-on experience allows IT and security teams to validate their incident detection and response procedures, identify gaps in their defense strategies, and prioritize improvements to mitigate future risks.

During the exercise, participants may execute CLI commands to analyze log files, conduct forensic investigations, or isolate affected systems. For example, IT administrators might use commands like `grep`, `awk`, or `tail` to search for specific patterns in log files and identify suspicious activities. Security analysts may utilize tools such as `tcpdump` or `Wireshark` to capture and analyze network traffic, uncovering potential indicators of an ongoing attack or unauthorized access attempts.

In addition to technical aspects, tabletop exercises emphasize the importance of effective communication and collaboration across departments. Participants practice communicating incident details, updates, and action plans through predefined communication channels, such as incident response platforms, email distributions, or conference calls. Clear and timely communication is essential for coordinating response efforts, managing stakeholder expectations, and maintaining transparency during a crisis.

Furthermore, tabletop exercises serve as a platform for testing crisis communication strategies and media relations protocols. Communications teams may draft press releases, prepare public statements, and engage with journalists or regulatory agencies as part of the simulated scenario. By practicing these scenarios, organizations can refine their messaging, manage reputational risks, and demonstrate accountability to customers, shareholders, and regulatory bodies.

Effective debriefing sessions are critical to maximizing the learning outcomes of tabletop exercises. Post-exercise discussions allow participants to reflect on their performance, identify strengths and weaknesses in their response efforts, and capture lessons learned for future improvements. Facilitators and observers provide constructive feedback and recommendations for enhancing incident response procedures, updating policies, or investing in additional training and resources.

Continuous improvement is a core principle of incident response tabletop exercises. Organizations should document insights, action items, and recommendations from each exercise to track progress over time and prioritize initiatives for enhancing their incident response capabilities. This iterative process ensures that incident response plans remain relevant and effective in addressing emerging threats and evolving regulatory requirements.

Moreover, tabletop exercises can be customized to simulate different levels of complexity and severity, ranging from minor security incidents to full-scale crises impacting business continuity. Advanced exercises may involve multiple stakeholders, including external partners, third-party vendors, and regulatory authorities, to test coordination and collaboration during a widespread incident. These comprehensive simulations help organizations assess their readiness to manage complex scenarios that could have far-reaching operational, financial, and reputational implications.

In summary, incident response tabletop exercises are essential tools for organizations seeking to strengthen their resilience against cyber threats and operational disruptions. By simulating realistic scenarios and testing response strategies, teams can identify and address vulnerabilities in their incident response plans, improve coordination across departments, and enhance their overall readiness to mitigate and recover from security incidents. Integrating tabletop exercises into regular training programs enables organizations to foster a culture of preparedness, continuous improvement, and effective crisis management.

BOOK 4
MASTERING CYBER INCIDENT RESPONSE:
COMPREHENSIVE TECHNIQUES FOR ELITE SECURITY
INVESTIGATORS

ROB BOTWRIGHT

Chapter 1: Strategic Planning for Incident Response

Developing incident response policies and procedures is a critical endeavor for any organization aiming to fortify its cybersecurity posture and resilience against potential threats. These policies serve as foundational documents that outline the organization's approach to detecting, responding to, and recovering from security incidents. The process typically begins with a comprehensive assessment of the organization's current cybersecurity landscape, including identifying assets, assessing risks, and understanding regulatory requirements that may influence policy development. A thorough understanding of the organization's infrastructure, systems, and data flows is essential to crafting effective policies that address specific threats and vulnerabilities.

One of the primary goals of developing incident response policies is to establish clear guidelines and responsibilities for personnel involved in incident handling. This includes defining roles such as incident responders, IT administrators, legal advisors, and communications specialists, each with distinct responsibilities during different phases of incident response. For instance, incident response policies may designate specific individuals or teams responsible for coordinating technical responses, communicating with stakeholders, and liaising with law enforcement or regulatory agencies if necessary.

Furthermore, incident response policies should outline the procedures for identifying and classifying security incidents based on their severity and potential impact on the organization. This classification helps prioritize response efforts and allocate resources effectively. Common incident classifications include phishing attacks, malware infections, unauthorized access attempts, denial-of-service incidents, and data breaches, each requiring tailored response strategies and escalation procedures.

Effective incident response policies also emphasize the importance of timely incident detection and notification. Organizations should implement monitoring tools and techniques such as intrusion detection systems (IDS), security information and event management (SIEM) systems, and endpoint detection and response (EDR) solutions to detect anomalies and potential security breaches. Incident detection techniques often involve analyzing network traffic logs, monitoring system alerts for suspicious activities, and deploying endpoint security agents to identify and quarantine malicious files or processes.

Once an incident is detected, incident response policies dictate the immediate actions and steps required to contain the threat and minimize its impact on the organization's operations. This may involve isolating affected systems or devices from the network, disabling compromised user accounts, or implementing temporary mitigations to prevent further exploitation.

CLI commands such as `netstat`, `ps`, or `tasklist` can be used to identify active network connections, running processes, and associated system resources to determine if unauthorized activities are occurring.

Moreover, incident response policies should include guidelines for conducting thorough investigations to determine the root cause and scope of the incident. This investigative process often involves collecting and preserving evidence, performing forensic analysis of compromised systems, and documenting findings to support remediation efforts and potential legal proceedings. CLI tools such as `dd`, `foremost`, or `Autopsy` can be utilized to create disk images, recover deleted files, and analyze filesystems for traces of malicious activity during forensic investigations.

Communication and coordination are critical aspects of incident response policies, emphasizing the need for clear and effective communication channels within the organization and with external stakeholders. Policies should outline protocols for internal notification and escalation procedures, ensuring that incident responders and management are promptly informed of ongoing incidents and their potential impact. Additionally, policies should define procedures for communicating with customers, partners, regulatory authorities, and the media to maintain transparency, manage reputational risks, and comply with legal obligations.

Furthermore, incident response policies should incorporate guidelines for assessing the impact of security incidents on the organization's operations, financial stability, and regulatory compliance. This impact assessment helps prioritize recovery efforts and determine the resources required to restore affected systems and services. Organizations may use incident response management platforms or incident tracking spreadsheets to document incident details, track response activities, and measure the overall effectiveness of their incident response efforts.

An essential component of developing incident response policies is establishing a framework for continuous improvement and learning from past incidents. Organizations should conduct post-incident reviews or "lessons learned" sessions to evaluate the effectiveness of response actions, identify gaps or deficiencies in policies and procedures, and implement corrective measures to prevent future incidents. These reviews provide valuable insights into recurring patterns of attacks, emerging threats, and areas where additional training or resources may be needed to enhance incident response capabilities.

Additionally, incident response policies should address the importance of compliance with relevant laws, regulations, and industry standards governing data protection, privacy, and incident reporting. Depending on the organization's jurisdiction and industry sector, policies may need to align with frameworks such as the

General Data Protection Regulation (GDPR), Health Insurance Portability and Accountability Act (HIPAA), or Payment Card Industry Data Security Standard (PCI DSS). Compliance with these regulations helps mitigate legal risks, avoid financial penalties, and maintain trust with customers and stakeholders.

Moreover, incident response policies should include provisions for regular testing and validation of incident response plans through tabletop exercises, simulated scenarios, or red teaming exercises. These proactive measures allow organizations to assess their readiness to respond to various types of security incidents, identify areas for improvement, and familiarize incident response teams with their roles and responsibilities in a controlled environment. Testing also helps build confidence in the effectiveness of incident response procedures and fosters a culture of preparedness across the organization.

In summary, developing comprehensive incident response policies and procedures is essential for organizations to mitigate cybersecurity risks, protect sensitive data, and maintain business continuity in the face of evolving threats. By establishing clear guidelines, defining roles and responsibilities, implementing effective detection and response mechanisms, and fostering a culture of continuous improvement, organizations can strengthen their resilience and readiness to respond to security incidents effectively. Integrating incident response policies into the overall cybersecurity framework ensures a coordinated and proactive approach to incident management, ultimately safeguarding the organization's reputation, assets, and stakeholder trust. Creating incident response playbooks is a crucial component of an organization's efforts to streamline and standardize its response to security incidents. These playbooks serve as comprehensive guides that outline predefined steps, procedures, and decision-making criteria for addressing specific types of incidents effectively. The process begins with identifying and prioritizing potential security threats and vulnerabilities that the organization may face, based on its industry, size, and regulatory environment. By understanding these factors, organizations can tailor their incident response playbooks to address the most relevant and impactful scenarios.

One of the primary objectives of creating incident response playbooks is to establish consistency and efficiency in incident handling procedures across the organization. Playbooks define the roles and responsibilities of incident response team members, including IT staff, security analysts, legal advisors, and communications personnel, ensuring clear accountability and coordination during incident response efforts. Each playbook typically includes detailed instructions, checklists, and decision trees that guide responders through the steps required to contain, investigate, mitigate, and recover from specific types of incidents.

Moreover, incident response playbooks should incorporate incident classification frameworks to categorize incidents based on their severity, impact, and potential consequences for the organization. Common incident classification schemes include the Common Vulnerability Scoring System (CVSS), which assesses vulnerabilities based on their exploitability and potential impact, and the Incident Severity Assessment Framework (ISAF), which categorizes incidents by their operational and financial impact on the organization. By classifying incidents appropriately, organizations can prioritize response efforts and allocate resources effectively to minimize disruptions and mitigate risks.

In addition to defining incident classification criteria, incident response playbooks should outline escalation procedures for escalating incidents to higher levels of management or involving external stakeholders, such as law enforcement, regulatory authorities, or third-party incident response teams. Clear escalation paths ensure that critical decisions are made promptly, response efforts are coordinated effectively, and appropriate resources are mobilized to address the incident's scope and complexity.

Furthermore, incident response playbooks should incorporate technical response procedures for identifying, containing, and eradicating security threats within the organization's IT infrastructure. These procedures often involve deploying security tools and technologies such as intrusion detection systems (IDS), endpoint detection and response (EDR) solutions, and network monitoring tools to detect anomalous activities, investigate suspicious behavior, and isolate compromised systems or devices. CLI commands such as `netstat`, `ps`, or `grep` can be used to analyze network connections, list running processes, and search for specific patterns or indicators of compromise (IOCs) on affected systems.

Additionally, incident response playbooks should include guidelines for preserving and analyzing digital evidence during forensic investigations to determine the root cause of the incident and support potential legal or disciplinary actions. Forensic analysis techniques may involve creating disk images, capturing volatile memory snapshots, and using forensic tools such as `dd`, `Autopsy`, or `EnCase` to recover deleted files and examine filesystems for traces of malicious activity. By documenting forensic procedures and best practices in playbooks, organizations can ensure that evidence is collected and handled in a manner that preserves its integrity and admissibility in legal proceedings.

Communication protocols are another essential component of incident response playbooks, outlining procedures for internal and external communication during a security incident. Playbooks should specify communication channels, contact information for key stakeholders and response team members, and templates for incident notifications, updates, and status reports. Effective communication ensures that stakeholders are informed promptly about the incident's impact, response efforts underway, and any actions they need to take to minimize further risks or disruptions.

Moreover, incident response playbooks should address post-incident activities and recovery procedures to restore affected systems, services, and data to normal operations. These procedures may include validating system backups, implementing patches or security updates to prevent future incidents, and conducting post-mortem reviews or "lessons learned" sessions to evaluate the effectiveness of response actions and identify areas for improvement in playbooks or incident response processes.

Continuous testing and refinement of incident response playbooks are essential to ensure their effectiveness and relevance in addressing evolving cybersecurity threats and organizational needs. Organizations should conduct tabletop exercises, simulated scenarios, or red teaming exercises to validate playbooks, assess response capabilities, and identify gaps or deficiencies in incident handling procedures. These exercises allow incident response teams to practice their roles and responsibilities, test decision-making processes, and refine communication and coordination strategies in a controlled environment.

Furthermore, incident response playbooks should be reviewed and updated regularly to reflect changes in the organization's IT environment, emerging threats, regulatory requirements, and lessons learned from previous incidents. By incorporating feedback from incident response exercises, incident reports, and security audits, organizations can enhance the comprehensiveness and effectiveness of their playbooks, ensuring they remain a valuable resource for incident responders and stakeholders.

In summary, creating effective incident response playbooks is essential for organizations to enhance their readiness and resilience against cybersecurity threats. By defining standardized procedures, roles, and responsibilities for incident handling, incorporating incident classification frameworks, outlining escalation and communication protocols, and detailing technical response and forensic investigation procedures, organizations can streamline their response efforts, minimize the impact of security incidents, and protect their assets, reputation, and stakeholder trust. Continuous testing, refinement, and updating of playbooks ensure they remain relevant and effective in addressing the evolving landscape of cyber threats and organizational requirements for incident response readiness.

Chapter 2: Advanced Threat Intelligence and Analysis

Threat hunting techniques represent proactive approaches employed by cybersecurity professionals to identify and mitigate potential threats that may evade traditional security measures. Unlike reactive incident response, threat hunting involves actively searching for signs of malicious activity or indicators of compromise (IOCs) within an organization's network, endpoints, and systems. The goal is to detect threats at an early stage before they can cause significant damage or exfiltrate sensitive data. Effective threat hunting requires a combination of advanced technical skills, knowledge of adversary tactics, techniques, and procedures (TTPs), and access to comprehensive threat intelligence sources.

One of the fundamental techniques in threat hunting involves analyzing network traffic to identify anomalous patterns or suspicious behaviors that may indicate unauthorized access or data exfiltration attempts. Network monitoring tools such as `tcpdump`, `Wireshark`, or `Suricata` can capture and analyze packets to detect unusual communication patterns, unexpected data transfers, or connections to known malicious IP addresses. By scrutinizing network logs and traffic metadata, threat hunters can uncover potential indicators of compromise and investigate further to determine the scope and impact of suspicious activities.

Endpoint detection and response (EDR) tools play a crucial role in threat hunting by providing real-time visibility into endpoint activities and enabling rapid detection of suspicious behavior or unauthorized system access. EDR solutions such as `Carbon Black`, `CrowdStrike Falcon`, or `Symantec Endpoint Protection` monitor endpoint events, processes, and file system activities to detect indicators of compromise (IOCs) and anomalous behaviors. Threat hunters can leverage EDR capabilities to conduct in-depth forensic analysis, quarantine infected endpoints, and contain the spread of malware or malicious activities across the organization's network.

Moreover, threat hunting techniques often involve analyzing system logs and event data from various sources, including servers, firewalls, and application logs, to detect abnormal activities or security events that may indicate a potential breach or intrusion. Security information and event management (SIEM) platforms such as `Splunk`, `QRadar`, or `LogRhythm` aggregate and correlate log data from multiple sources to identify patterns, trends, and anomalies that could signify malicious behavior. Threat hunters can create custom queries, filters, and alerts within SIEM platforms to prioritize alerts and investigate potential security incidents promptly.

Another effective technique in threat hunting is leveraging threat intelligence feeds and external sources to enrich internal security data and enhance the detection capabilities of cybersecurity defenses. Threat intelligence platforms such as `ThreatConnect`, `Anomali`, or `FireEye iSIGHT` provide up-to-date information on known threats, vulnerabilities, and attack campaigns observed globally. By integrating threat intelligence feeds into their security infrastructure, organizations can proactively identify emerging threats, understand adversary tactics, and prioritize threat hunting efforts based on the likelihood and potential impact of specific threats.

Furthermore, conducting memory analysis and volatile data forensics is a critical aspect of advanced threat hunting techniques, especially for detecting stealthy and memory-resident malware or advanced persistent threats (APTs). Memory forensics tools such as `Volatility`, `Rekall`, or `Mandiant Redline` enable threat hunters to analyze memory dumps, process memory, and registry hives to identify malicious processes, injected code, or persistence mechanisms that may evade traditional antivirus solutions. By examining memory artifacts, threat hunters can uncover hidden malware, command-and-control (C2) communications, or evidence of privilege escalation attempts within compromised systems.

Additionally, threat hunting techniques may involve using deception technologies and honeypots to lure and trap adversaries attempting to infiltrate the organization's network or systems. Honeypots simulate vulnerable systems, services, or applications designed to attract and divert attackers away from critical assets. Tools such as `Kippo`, `Cowrie`, or `Modern Honey Network (MHN)` deploy honeypots to monitor and capture malicious activities, collect threat intelligence, and gather insights into adversary tactics and techniques. Threat hunters can analyze honeypot interactions and behaviors to identify new attack vectors, understand attacker motivations, and improve defensive strategies.

Moreover, leveraging behavioral analytics and machine learning algorithms can enhance threat hunting capabilities by identifying deviations from normal behavior patterns and detecting anomalies indicative of potential security threats. Behavioral analytics platforms such as `Darktrace`, `Vectra AI`, or `Exabeam` utilize machine learning models to establish baseline behaviors for users, devices, and applications within the organization's network. By continuously monitoring and analyzing behavioral deviations, these platforms can detect suspicious activities, insider threats, or unauthorized access attempts that may evade signature-based detection methods.

In addition to technical techniques, effective threat hunting requires collaboration and knowledge sharing among cybersecurity teams, threat intelligence analysts, incident responders, and stakeholders across the organization. Collaborative threat hunting exercises, such as tabletop simulations or red team engagements, enable teams to practice coordinated responses to simulated attack scenarios, validate incident response playbooks, and strengthen communication and coordination during crisis situations. These exercises foster a proactive security culture, enhance team readiness, and improve overall incident response capabilities.

Furthermore, threat hunting should be an iterative and adaptive process that evolves alongside emerging threats, technological advancements, and organizational changes. Regularly updating threat hunting strategies, tools, and procedures based on lessons learned from previous incidents, threat intelligence insights, and industry best practices ensures that organizations remain agile and effective in detecting and mitigating evolving cyber threats. Continuous training and skills development for threat hunters are essential to stay abreast of new attack vectors, techniques, and defensive technologies in the ever-changing cybersecurity landscape.

In summary, effective threat hunting techniques empower organizations to detect and respond to cybersecurity threats proactively, minimize potential damage, and safeguard sensitive data and critical assets. By leveraging advanced tools and technologies, analyzing network traffic, endpoint activities, system logs, and leveraging threat intelligence feeds, organizations can enhance their detection capabilities, identify potential threats early, and mitigate risks before they escalate. Collaboration, continuous improvement, and adaptive strategies are key to maintaining a robust threat hunting program that aligns with organizational goals and protects against evolving cyber threats effectively. Threat intelligence sharing and collaboration are essential practices in the cybersecurity community aimed at enhancing collective defense capabilities, improving incident response times, and mitigating the impact of cyber threats across organizations and sectors. These practices involve the exchange of actionable information about emerging threats, indicators of compromise (IOCs), malicious activities, and adversary tactics, techniques, and procedures (TTPs) among trusted partners, industry peers, government agencies, and cybersecurity vendors. By sharing timely and relevant threat intelligence, organizations can proactively identify and address potential security risks before they manifest into full-blown incidents or breaches.

One of the primary benefits of threat intelligence sharing is its role in strengthening the overall cybersecurity posture of participating organizations through collaborative defense strategies. By pooling resources, expertise, and threat insights, organizations can gain a broader and more comprehensive view of the threat landscape, enabling them to detect and respond to threats more effectively. This collective approach helps identify common attack patterns, vulnerabilities, and attack vectors that adversaries may exploit across multiple targets within the same industry or geographical region.

Furthermore, threat intelligence sharing fosters a proactive security culture by promoting information exchange on emerging threats, zero-day vulnerabilities, and new attack techniques that may not yet be widely known or mitigated by existing security controls. This proactive stance allows organizations to preemptively update their defenses, implement patches or security updates, and adjust their incident response strategies to mitigate potential risks before they impact their operations or compromise sensitive data.

Effective threat intelligence sharing relies on establishing trusted relationships and partnerships with peers, industry groups, information sharing and analysis centers (ISACs), and government agencies. These partnerships facilitate the secure and confidential exchange of sensitive information while adhering to legal and regulatory requirements governing data privacy, confidentiality, and intellectual property protection. Trusted platforms and forums, such as threat intelligence sharing communities, collaboration portals, or secure email exchanges, provide secure channels for sharing threat data and fostering mutual trust among participants.

Moreover, automated threat intelligence platforms and sharing frameworks play a crucial role in streamlining the exchange and dissemination of threat information among stakeholders. These platforms aggregate, normalize, and correlate threat data from various sources, including internal security logs, external threat feeds, and community contributions, to provide actionable insights and indicators that can be integrated into existing security technologies and workflows. Examples of such platforms include `MISP (Malware Information Sharing Platform)`, `STIX/TAXII

(Structured Threat Information Expression / Trusted Automated Exchange of Intelligence Information)`, and `OpenDXL (Open Data Exchange Layer)`.

In addition to sharing technical indicators such as IP addresses, domain names, and file hashes, threat intelligence collaboration also includes contextual information about threat actors, their motives, tactics, and observed behaviors. This contextual understanding helps organizations prioritize threats based on their relevance and potential impact, allocate resources effectively, and tailor their defensive strategies to mitigate specific adversary tactics and techniques. Analysts and incident responders can leverage this contextual intelligence to conduct more targeted investigations, identify patterns of malicious activity across different attack campaigns, and attribute incidents to specific threat actors or cybercriminal groups.

Furthermore, threat intelligence sharing supports threat hunting and proactive defense initiatives by providing organizations with early warnings and insights into emerging threats and attack trends. Threat hunters can use shared intelligence to search for traces of known IOCs, anomalous behaviors, or indicators of advanced persistent threats (APTs) within their networks and systems. This proactive approach enables organizations to detect and disrupt potential attacks at an early stage, reducing the likelihood of successful compromises and minimizing the impact on business operations.

Additionally, threat intelligence collaboration extends beyond technical indicators and includes strategic insights and best practices for enhancing cybersecurity resilience and incident response readiness. Participating organizations can share lessons learned from past incidents, case studies, and recommended mitigation strategies to help peers strengthen their defenses and improve their incident response capabilities. This knowledge sharing fosters a culture of continuous improvement, where organizations learn from each other's experiences and adapt their security strategies to address evolving threats effectively.

Moreover, threat intelligence sharing plays a crucial role in supporting regulatory compliance and industry-specific security requirements. Many regulatory frameworks, such as the General Data Protection Regulation (GDPR), Payment Card Industry Data Security Standard (PCI DSS), and healthcare regulations like the Health Insurance Portability and Accountability Act (HIPAA), emphasize the importance of information sharing and collaboration to enhance cybersecurity resilience and protect sensitive data. By participating in threat intelligence sharing initiatives, organizations demonstrate their commitment to regulatory compliance and proactive risk management, thereby mitigating legal and financial risks associated with data breaches and security incidents.

To facilitate effective threat intelligence sharing and collaboration, organizations should establish clear policies, guidelines, and procedures for participating in information sharing communities, exchanging sensitive information, and adhering to legal and ethical standards. These policies should address data privacy and confidentiality concerns, define roles and responsibilities for sharing and receiving threat intelligence, and establish mechanisms for verifying the credibility and accuracy of shared information. Regular training and awareness programs for employees involved in threat intelligence activities help promote best practices, encourage responsible information sharing, and mitigate potential risks associated with data leakage or misuse.

In summary, threat intelligence sharing and collaboration are integral components of a proactive cybersecurity strategy that enables organizations to detect, respond to, and mitigate cyber threats effectively. By fostering trusted partnerships, leveraging automated sharing platforms, exchanging actionable threat data, and sharing strategic insights and best practices, organizations can enhance their collective defense capabilities, improve incident response times, and reduce the impact of cyber incidents on their operations and stakeholders. Continuous engagement in threat intelligence sharing initiatives contributes to a resilient cybersecurity ecosystem where information exchange and collaboration play a pivotal role in safeguarding critical infrastructure, sensitive data, and maintaining trust in digital ecosystems.

Chapter 3: Incident Response Team Organization and Management

Building and training an incident response team is a critical initiative for organizations aiming to strengthen their cybersecurity posture and readiness to effectively manage and mitigate security incidents. The process begins with identifying key stakeholders and assembling a multidisciplinary team comprising individuals with specialized skills and expertise in areas such as IT security, network forensics, digital forensics, incident handling, legal compliance, and communications. Each team member plays a crucial role in different phases of incident response, from detection and containment to investigation, remediation, and recovery.

To build an effective incident response team, organizations should define clear roles, responsibilities, and reporting structures for team members, ensuring accountability and coordination during incident response activities. Key roles typically include incident responders who handle technical aspects such as analyzing security alerts, investigating compromised systems, and implementing containment measures using commands like `netstat`, `ps`, or `grep` to identify suspicious processes or network connections. These responders work closely with IT administrators to isolate affected systems, mitigate ongoing threats, and restore normal operations while preserving digital evidence for forensic analysis.

Moreover, organizations should designate a team leader or incident commander responsible for overseeing the overall incident response process, coordinating communication with senior management, legal advisors, and external stakeholders, and making strategic decisions to prioritize response efforts and resource allocation during a security incident. The incident commander plays a pivotal role in maintaining situational awareness, managing incident response workflows, and ensuring adherence to established incident response policies, playbooks, and regulatory requirements.

In addition to technical expertise, incident response teams benefit from cross-functional collaboration and diverse perspectives that enhance their ability to address complex and multifaceted security incidents effectively. Legal advisors provide guidance on data privacy laws, regulatory compliance requirements, and incident reporting obligations, helping organizations navigate legal implications and mitigate legal risks associated with data breaches or security incidents. Communication specialists play a crucial role in managing internal and external communications, preparing public statements, and maintaining transparency with stakeholders, customers, and regulatory authorities throughout the incident lifecycle.

Furthermore, building an incident response team involves establishing effective communication channels, escalation procedures, and response workflows to ensure timely notification, decision-making, and action during security incidents. Incident response platforms such as `ServiceNow Security Incident Response`, `IBM Resilient`, or `Atlassian Jira` facilitate incident coordination, task assignment, and tracking of response activities, enabling team members to collaborate seamlessly and maintain visibility into incident response progress. These platforms also support incident documentation, evidence collection, and post-incident analysis to facilitate continuous improvement of incident response processes.

Training and continuous skills development are essential components of building a proficient incident response team capable of responding swiftly and effectively to evolving cybersecurity threats. Organizations should invest in regular training exercises, workshops, and certifications to enhance team members' technical proficiency in incident detection, response techniques, digital forensics, and threat intelligence analysis. Hands-on training scenarios, such as tabletop exercises or simulated cyber attack simulations, allow teams to practice incident response procedures in a controlled environment, test their knowledge of playbooks, and refine their coordination and communication skills under pressure.

Additionally, organizations can leverage external resources, such as industry conferences, cybersecurity workshops, and professional associations like the SANS

Institute or ISC2, to access specialized training programs, certification courses, and expert-led seminars on incident response best practices and emerging threats. Continuous skills development ensures that incident response teams stay abreast of new attack vectors, evolving adversary tactics, and advancements in cybersecurity technologies, enabling them to adapt their response strategies and techniques accordingly.

Furthermore, fostering a culture of collaboration and knowledge sharing within the incident response team and across the organization enhances team cohesion and collective problem-solving capabilities. Regular debriefings, post-mortem reviews, and knowledge-sharing sessions following security incidents help identify lessons learned, strengths, and areas for improvement in incident response processes, playbooks, and communication protocols. Cross-training team members in different roles or disciplines within incident response also promotes versatility and resilience, enabling teams to fill gaps during personnel shortages or escalating incidents.

Moreover, organizations should establish metrics and key performance indicators (KPIs) to measure the effectiveness of their incident response team and continuously evaluate their performance against predefined benchmarks. Metrics such as mean time to detect (MTTD), mean time to respond (MTTR), and incident closure rates provide insights into response efficiency, detection capabilities, and operational readiness to mitigate security incidents promptly. Regular review of incident response metrics enables organizations to identify bottlenecks, refine response workflows, and allocate resources more effectively to enhance overall incident response effectiveness.

Additionally, building an incident response team involves cultivating relationships with external partners, including law enforcement agencies, incident response vendors, managed security service providers (MSSPs), and industry-specific information sharing and analysis centers (ISACs). These partnerships facilitate access to threat intelligence, forensic expertise, and specialized resources during complex investigations or large-scale security incidents. Collaborating with external stakeholders also enhances incident response capabilities, expands access to industry insights and best practices, and strengthens the organization's resilience against sophisticated cyber threats.

In summary, building and training an incident response team is a strategic investment for organizations seeking to strengthen their cybersecurity defenses, mitigate risks, and maintain business continuity in the face of increasing cyber threats. By assembling a skilled and multidisciplinary team, defining clear roles and responsibilities, implementing effective communication channels and response workflows, and investing in continuous training and skills development, organizations can enhance their incident response readiness and resilience. Continuous evaluation, collaboration with external partners, and adherence to incident response best practices ensure that incident response teams remain adaptive, proactive, and effective in protecting critical assets, mitigating security incidents, and safeguarding stakeholder trustIncident Command System (ICS) implementation is a structured approach used by organizations to manage and coordinate response efforts during emergencies, incidents, or crises effectively. Originally developed by fire services in the United States, ICS has evolved into a widely adopted framework across various industries, including emergency management, law enforcement, healthcare, and corporate environments, due to its scalability, flexibility, and standardized approach to incident management. The primary objective of ICS is to establish a hierarchical command structure, define clear roles and responsibilities, facilitate communication, and streamline decision-making processes to achieve efficient and coordinated response operations.

The foundation of ICS implementation lies in establishing a clear organizational structure comprising key positions and roles that align with incident management principles. At the core of ICS is the Incident Commander (IC), who assumes overall responsibility for managing the incident, making strategic decisions, and ensuring the safety of personnel and resources involved. The IC is typically appointed based on experience, expertise, and authority within the organization, and is responsible for declaring an incident, assessing the situation, and initiating response actions.

To deploy ICS effectively, organizations designate Incident Command Staff (ICS) positions such as Operations Section Chief, Planning Section Chief, Logistics Section Chief, and Finance/Administration Section Chief, depending on the size, complexity, and nature of the incident. Each section chief oversees specific functional areas: the Operations Section Chief directs tactical response activities and resource allocation, the Planning Section Chief manages situation assessment, resource planning, and documentation using tools like `ICS Form 201` to capture incident objectives and `ICS Form 202` to document incident briefing, while the Logistics Section Chief coordinates resource procurement, distribution, and support services, ensuring personnel have access to necessary equipment and supplies through commands such as `ICS Form 204` for tracking resources and `ICS Form 205` for incident radio communications plan.

Chapter 4: Advanced Forensic Investigation Techniques

Memory forensics and volatility analysis represent advanced techniques in digital forensics used to investigate and analyze volatile memory (RAM) of computer systems for traces of malicious activities, unauthorized access, or cyber attacks. Unlike traditional disk-based forensics, which focuses on examining storage devices for evidence, memory forensics involves capturing and analyzing the contents of a system's RAM to uncover artifacts, processes, network connections, and other volatile data that may not be accessible through disk-based analysis alone. This approach is particularly valuable in detecting stealthy malware, rootkits, and memory-resident threats that evade detection by antivirus software or leave minimal traces on disk.

The process of conducting memory forensics begins with acquiring a memory dump or snapshot of the target system's RAM using tools such as `DumpIt`, `Magnet RAM Capture`, or `FTK Imager`. These tools capture the volatile memory contents at a specific point in time, preserving the state of running processes, loaded modules, network connections, and other system artifacts crucial for forensic analysis. Once the memory dump is acquired, forensic investigators can analyze it using specialized tools and techniques to extract relevant information and identify indicators of compromise (IOCs) or suspicious activities.

One of the primary tools used for memory forensics and volatility analysis is `Volatility`, an open-source framework designed for extracting digital artifacts from memory dumps. `Volatility` supports various operating systems and architectures, including Windows, Linux, macOS, and Android, and offers a wide range of plugins for analyzing memory artifacts related to processes, network connections, registry hives, file system metadata, and more. Analysts can use `Volatility` commands such as `volatility imageinfo` to determine the profile of the memory dump, `volatility pslist` to list running processes, `volatility connections` to examine network connections, and `volatility timeliner` to create a timeline of system activity based on memory artifacts.

Moreover, `Volatility` plugins such as `malfind` can detect and analyze suspicious code injection or process hollowing techniques used by malware to hide its presence in memory. Similarly, the `filescan` plugin scans memory for file handles and metadata, allowing analysts to identify files accessed or manipulated by malicious processes. By correlating these findings with other forensic evidence and incident data, investigators can reconstruct the sequence of events leading to a security incident, identify the root cause of a compromise, and attribute malicious activities to specific threat actors or malware families.

Furthermore, memory forensics techniques enable analysts to recover artifacts such as passwords, encryption keys, and sensitive data stored in memory during a security incident. Tools like `Volatility` can parse memory structures related to browser sessions, instant messaging applications, and encryption libraries to extract credentials, session tokens, and cryptographic keys used for data encryption or secure communications. This capability is particularly valuable in cases involving data breaches, insider threats, or unauthorized access attempts where identifying compromised credentials or encryption keys is critical for mitigating further risks and securing affected systems.

In addition to `Volatility`, other commercial and open-source memory forensics tools such as `Rekall`, `Mandiant Redline`, and `WinPMEM` offer complementary features and capabilities for analyzing memory dumps and conducting advanced volatility analysis. These tools provide graphical user interfaces (GUIs), command-line interfaces (CLIs), and scripting capabilities to automate memory analysis tasks, perform bulk processing of memory dumps, and generate detailed reports for forensic investigations and incident response activities.

Moreover, memory forensics and volatility analysis play a crucial role in incident response by providing real-time insights into ongoing security incidents, enabling rapid detection, containment, and mitigation of memory-resident threats. During incident response operations, forensic analysts may use live memory analysis techniques, such as `LiME` (Linux Memory Extractor) or `WinPmem`, to acquire memory dumps from live systems without disrupting normal operations. Live memory analysis allows investigators to capture volatile data associated with active processes, network connections, and system states, facilitating immediate response actions to stop ongoing attacks and preserve forensic evidence.

Additionally, memory forensics techniques support digital investigations across a wide range of cybersecurity incidents, including malware infections, data breaches, insider threats, ransomware attacks, and advanced persistent threats (APTs). By analyzing memory dumps from compromised systems, investigators can reconstruct attack timelines, identify attack vectors, and determine the extent of unauthorized access or data exfiltration. This forensic evidence is crucial for understanding attacker tactics, techniques, and procedures (TTPs), attributing incidents to specific threat actors or groups, and developing effective mitigation strategies to prevent future attacks.

Furthermore, memory forensics is instrumental in supporting regulatory compliance requirements and legal proceedings by providing verifiable evidence of security incidents, data breaches, or unauthorized access incidents. Forensic analysts can document findings from memory dumps, including timestamps, process execution paths, and system configurations, to demonstrate compliance with data protection laws, industry regulations, and incident reporting obligations. This forensic evidence strengthens organizations' ability to respond to regulatory inquiries, cooperate with law enforcement agencies, and mitigate legal and financial risks associated with cybersecurity incidents.

In summary, memory forensics and volatility analysis represent indispensable techniques in modern digital forensics and incident response practices, enabling organizations to uncover hidden threats, identify malicious activities, and mitigate the impact of cybersecurity incidents effectively. By leveraging tools like `Volatility`, `Rekall`, and `WinPMEM`, forensic analysts can acquire, analyze, and interpret memory dumps to extract valuable artifacts, detect indicators of compromise (IOCs), and support comprehensive investigations across diverse cybersecurity incidents. Continuous advancements in memory forensics tools and techniques empower organizations to enhance their incident response capabilities, strengthen their cybersecurity defenses, and safeguard critical assets against evolving threats in today's dynamic threat landscape. Data recovery techniques in forensics encompass a range of methodologies and tools used to retrieve, reconstruct, and analyze digital information from storage devices such as hard drives, solid-state drives (SSDs), USB drives, and memory cards. These techniques are essential for forensic investigations aimed at recovering deleted files, reconstructing damaged data, and extracting evidence from compromised or inaccessible storage media. The process of data recovery in forensic investigations typically begins with acquiring a forensic image or bit-by-bit copy of the storage device using tools like `dd`, `dc3dd`, or `FTK Imager`, which create a forensically sound copy of the original data while preserving its integrity and chain of custody.

Once a forensic image is acquired, forensic examiners use specialized tools and techniques to analyze the image and recover potentially relevant data. File carving is a fundamental data recovery technique that involves scanning the forensic image for file headers, footers, and data patterns to extract intact files and fragments that may have been deleted or overwritten. Tools such as `Foremost`, `Scalpel`, or `PhotoRec` are commonly used for file carving in forensic investigations, allowing examiners to recover deleted documents, images, videos, and other file types based on predefined file signatures and data structures.

In addition to file carving, forensic examiners employ disk imaging and cloning techniques to create exact replicas or clones of storage devices for offline analysis and data recovery. Tools like `dd` (Disk Dump) command can be used to create a bit-by-bit copy of the original disk or partition, while tools such as `ddrescue` or `Clonezilla` facilitate the cloning process by handling bad sectors, read errors, and other disk anomalies to ensure complete and accurate data replication. Disk imaging and cloning are critical for preserving evidence integrity, conducting parallel forensic examinations, and performing data recovery operations without altering or compromising the original storage media.

Moreover, data recovery techniques in forensic investigations include logical and physical data acquisition methods tailored to different types of storage devices and file systems. Logical acquisition involves extracting files and metadata from the file system level using tools like `Encase`, `FTK Imager`, or `AccessData FTK`, which can acquire data from live systems or mounted storage devices while preserving file attributes and timestamps for forensic analysis. Physical acquisition, on the other hand, involves acquiring a lower-level sector-by-sector copy of the entire storage device, bypassing the file system and capturing all data, including deleted files and unallocated space, using commands like `dd` or specialized hardware write blockers and forensic acquisition devices.

Furthermore, data recovery techniques in forensic investigations extend to recovering data from damaged, corrupted, or encrypted storage media through advanced forensic analysis and data reconstruction methods. When encountering damaged or physically compromised storage devices, forensic examiners may use specialized hardware tools and techniques to repair or stabilize the device, recover readable sectors, and extract accessible data using `TestDisk`, `R-Studio`, or `GetDataBack` to perform in-depth data recovery from damaged or corrupted storage media.

In cases involving encrypted storage media or files protected by encryption algorithms, forensic examiners utilize forensic decryption techniques to recover plaintext data from encrypted data containers or files. Tools such as `Passware Kit Forensic`, `Encase`, or `AccessData FTK` support forensic decryption of password-protected files, encrypted volumes, and encrypted communications by employing brute-force attacks, dictionary attacks, or leveraging known vulnerabilities in encryption algorithms. Forensic decryption techniques require specialized knowledge of cryptography, encryption standards, and password cracking methods to successfully recover and analyze encrypted data in forensic investigations.

Moreover, data recovery techniques in forensic investigations include reconstructing fragmented files and data structures from storage devices where files are fragmented across multiple sectors or clusters. Fragmented file recovery tools like `R-Studio`, `GetDataBack`, or `Scalpel` analyze the file system metadata and allocate chains to reconstruct complete files from fragmented data blocks scattered across the storage device. By reconstructing fragmented files, forensic examiners can recover intact documents, images, databases, and other file types that may have been fragmented due to disk fragmentation, file system errors, or deliberate attempts to conceal data.

Additionally, data recovery techniques in forensic investigations encompass mobile device forensics, which involve extracting and analyzing data from smartphones, tablets, and other mobile devices to recover deleted messages, call logs, photos, videos, and application data. Mobile forensic tools such as `Cellebrite UFED`, `XRY`, or `Oxygen Forensic Detective` support logical and physical acquisition of mobile device data, bypassing device locks, and recovering data from internal storage, SIM cards, and external memory cards using specialized cables, adapters, or forensic boot loaders to initiate data extraction and analysis.

Furthermore, data recovery techniques in forensic investigations extend to cloud forensics, which involve acquiring, analyzing, and recovering digital evidence stored in cloud-based services and platforms. Cloud forensic tools such as `Magnet AXIOM`, `AccessData FTK`, or `Paraben E3` support forensic acquisition of data from cloud storage services like Dropbox, Google Drive, and Microsoft OneDrive, allowing examiners to recover files, metadata, sharing activities, and user interactions stored in the cloud using API-based or web-based authentication methods to access cloud data and analyze data objects stored in cloud environments

Chapter 5: Incident Response in Complex Networks

Network traffic analysis and packet inspection are fundamental techniques in cybersecurity and digital forensics used to monitor, analyze, and investigate the flow of data packets across computer networks for security incidents, performance monitoring, and troubleshooting purposes. This process involves capturing and examining network traffic in real-time or from stored packet captures to identify anomalies, detect malicious activities, and gain insights into network behavior and communication patterns. Tools such as `Wireshark`, `tcpdump`, and `tshark` are commonly used for network traffic analysis and packet inspection, enabling analysts to capture packets, filter traffic based on protocols or IP addresses using commands like `tcpdump -i eth0` to capture packets from interface eth0 or `tshark -r capture.pcap -Y 'http.request.method == POST'` to filter packets in a capture file for HTTP POST requests.

Network traffic analysis begins with the deployment of network monitoring solutions, such as `Snort`, `Suricata`, or `Security Onion`, which capture and log network packets passing through network interfaces, switches, or routers for real-time analysis and detection of suspicious or unauthorized activities. These tools employ intrusion detection and prevention techniques to inspect packet headers and payloads, compare traffic against predefined rulesets, and generate alerts or notifications for anomalous behavior, potential security threats, or policy violations using commands like `suricata -c /etc/suricata/suricata.yaml -i eth0` to start Suricata IDS on interface eth0 or `securityonion-nsm -r 2022-06-25-17-15-50` to review network traffic recorded by Security Onion.

Furthermore, packet inspection techniques involve analyzing individual packets within a network capture to extract metadata, payloads, and protocol headers for forensic analysis and incident response. Tools like `Wireshark`, `tcpdump`, or `tshark` facilitate deep packet inspection using filters such as `tcp.port == 443` to filter packets for TCP traffic on port 443 or `ip.src == 192.168.1.100` to filter packets originating from IP address 192.168.1.100 in a network capture file, enabling analysts to examine packet contents, decode protocols, and reconstruct network conversations to identify communication patterns or suspicious activities.

Moreover, network traffic analysis supports protocol analysis and anomaly detection by examining network packets for deviations from expected behavior or protocol specifications. Analysts can use tools like `Wireshark` or `tcpdump` with protocol dissectors and decoders to analyze protocol-specific traffic patterns, validate protocol compliance, and detect abnormalities such as malformed packets, protocol violations, or unauthorized protocol usage within the network using commands like `wireshark -r capture.pcap -Y 'ip.addr == 192.168.1.1 && http.request.method == GET'` to filter HTTP GET requests from IP address 192.168.1.1 in a capture file or `tcpdump -i eth0 icmp` to capture ICMP (Ping) packets on interface eth0.

Additionally, network traffic analysis enables forensic investigators to reconstruct network sessions and identify the source and destination of network communications, including communication timelines, data transfer volumes, and interaction patterns between hosts. Tools like `tshark` or `tcpflow` facilitate session reconstruction and stream reassembly by extracting and concatenating related packets based on session identifiers or sequence numbers, enabling analysts to reconstruct email conversations, file transfers, or VoIP calls from network captures using commands like `tshark -r capture.pcap -z follow,tcp,ascii,1` to follow TCP stream 1 and display ASCII content or `tcpflow -r capture.pcap -o output_dir` to reconstruct TCP flows from a capture file into separate files in output_dir.

Furthermore, network traffic analysis supports malware analysis and digital forensics investigations by identifying command-and-control (C2) communications, data exfiltration attempts, and malicious network behaviors associated with malware infections or compromised systems. Analysts can use network traffic analysis tools to identify suspicious domains, IP addresses, or network patterns indicative of malware activity, and analyze packet payloads, DNS queries, or HTTP requests for signs of malicious intent using commands like `tshark -r capture.pcap -Y 'dns.qry.name contains "malicious-domain.com"'` to filter DNS queries for a specific domain name in a capture file or `tcpdump -i eth0 -w capture.pcap 'port 443'` to capture HTTPS (SSL/TLS) traffic on interface eth0 for analysis.

Moreover, network traffic analysis supports incident response by providing real-time visibility into network activities, enabling rapid detection, containment, and mitigation of security incidents or data breaches. Analysts can use network traffic analysis tools to monitor network traffic for unauthorized access attempts, abnormal traffic patterns, or network-based attacks, and correlate findings with other security telemetry to prioritize response actions and mitigate ongoing threats using commands like `tshark -i eth0 -Y 'tcp.flags.syn == 1 && tcp.flags.ack == 0'` to capture

259

TCP SYN packets on interface eth0 or `securityonion-cp /nsm/sensor_data/1234-5678-9012-3456/2022-06-25/2022-06-25-17-15-50.pcap /mnt/forensics` to copy a network capture file to a forensic analysis workstation.

Additionally, network traffic analysis techniques support regulatory compliance and legal investigations by providing verifiable evidence of network activities, data transfers, and communication patterns. Forensic analysts can document findings from network traffic analysis, including timestamps, packet metadata, and protocol details, to demonstrate compliance with data protection laws, industry regulations, and incident reporting requirements using tools like `Zeek` (formerly known as `Bro`) to generate detailed network traffic logs or `Moloch` to capture, index, and analyze large volumes of network traffic for retrospective analysis and forensic investigations. Endpoint Detection and Response (EDR) solutions have become indispensable in modern cybersecurity strategies, especially in complex environments where organizations face diverse and sophisticated cyber threats. EDR platforms are designed to monitor, detect, investigate, and respond to security incidents across endpoints such as desktops, laptops, servers, mobile devices, and virtual machines, providing real-time visibility into endpoint activities and enhancing incident response capabilities. The deployment of EDR solutions begins with agent installation on endpoints, which involves deploying lightweight software agents such as `CrowdStrike Falcon`, `Carbon Black`, or `Microsoft Defender for Endpoint` using deployment tools like `Group Policy` for Windows environments or `Ansible` for automated deployment across Linux servers or workstations.

Once installed, EDR agents continuously monitor endpoint activities, collecting telemetry data such as process executions, file modifications, network connections, and system events to detect suspicious behaviors or indicators of compromise (IOCs). Analysts can leverage EDR platforms' centralized management consoles to configure agent policies, monitor endpoint health, and review security alerts generated by behavioral analytics, machine learning models, or threat intelligence feeds using `CrowdStrike Falcon` console to review security alerts or `Carbon Black` dashboard to monitor endpoint activities and threat detections.

Furthermore, EDR solutions utilize advanced detection capabilities, including signature-based detection, heuristic analysis, and behavioral analytics, to identify and prioritize potential threats based on their severity, impact, and likelihood of compromise. Analysts can use EDR commands like `mquery` in `CrowdStrike Falcon` or `cbquery` in `Carbon Black` to perform queries and searches across endpoints for specific indicators of compromise (IOCs), suspicious file hashes, or anomalous behaviors identified during threat hunting activities, allowing for detailed investigation and response using `mquery "process_name:malicious.exe"` to search for processes named "malicious.exe" or `cbquery process where process_name = "suspicious_process.exe"` to query Carbon Black for details on a suspicious process.

Moreover, EDR platforms facilitate incident response by providing automated response actions and remediation capabilities to contain and mitigate threats across endpoints in real-time. Security teams can use EDR tools to isolate compromised endpoints from the network, terminate malicious processes, delete or quarantine malicious files, and apply security patches or configuration changes using commands like `CrowdStrike Falcon` to isolate a compromised endpoint or `Carbon Black` to quarantine a suspicious file across multiple endpoints in the environment.

Additionally, EDR solutions support threat hunting initiatives by enabling proactive detection and investigation of potential security threats or indicators of compromise (IOCs) that evade traditional security defenses. Threat hunters leverage EDR platforms' query languages, such as `Falcon Query Language (FQL)` or `Carbon Black Query Language (CBQL)`, to search for patterns of suspicious behavior, unauthorized access attempts, or lateral movement across endpoints using commands like `FQL "process_name:cmd.exe and netconn_count:>10"` to query for instances of cmd.exe with more than 10 network connections or `CBQL process where process_name = "powershell.exe" and netconn_count > 5` to search for PowerShell processes with more than 5 network connections.

Furthermore, EDR solutions enhance visibility and forensic capabilities by providing detailed endpoint telemetry and historical data logs that enable analysts to reconstruct incident timelines, trace attack vectors, and perform root cause analysis for security incidents or data breaches using `CrowdStrike Falcon` to retrieve historical endpoint data or `Carbon Black` to analyze endpoint events and generate forensic reports based on detailed endpoint telemetry and historical activity logs.

Moreover, EDR solutions integrate with Security Information and Event Management (SIEM) platforms such as `Splunk`, `QRadar`, or `ArcSight` to correlate endpoint telemetry with network logs, security events, and threat intelligence feeds for comprehensive threat detection and response across the entire IT environment using `Splunk` queries to correlate EDR alerts with network traffic logs or `QRadar` rules to generate offenses based on combined EDR and SIEM data for enhanced visibility and threat detection capabilities.

Additionally, EDR solutions address compliance requirements by providing audit trails, reporting capabilities, and forensic evidence collection to support regulatory compliance audits, incident response investigations, and legal proceedings using `CrowdStrike Falcon` to generate compliance reports or `Carbon Black` to collect forensic evidence and preserve chain of custody for regulatory purposes.

Furthermore, EDR solutions are scalable and adaptable to meet the needs of complex environments with diverse operating systems, cloud services, and IoT devices, supporting centralized management, policy enforcement, and threat intelligence integration across distributed endpoints using `CrowdStrike Falcon` to manage multi-tenant environments or `Carbon Black` to deploy agents across hybrid cloud environments and remote endpoints using automation tools like Ansible or Puppet for consistent deployment and configuration management.

In summary, EDR solutions play a pivotal role in enhancing cybersecurity posture and incident response capabilities in complex environments by providing real-time visibility, advanced detection and response capabilities, proactive threat hunting, forensic analysis, and compliance support across diverse endpoints and IT infrastructures. The integration of EDR platforms with SIEM solutions, automation tools, and threat intelligence feeds enables organizations to detect, respond to, and mitigate evolving cyber threats effectively, safeguarding critical assets, maintaining regulatory compliance, and ensuring resilience against sophisticated cyber attacks in today's dynamic threat landscape.

Chapter 6: Continuous Monitoring and Threat Hunting

Implementing Security Information and Event Management (SIEM) systems is crucial for organizations seeking to enhance their cybersecurity posture by centralizing the collection, analysis, and correlation of security-related data from various sources across their IT infrastructure. SIEM platforms aggregate and normalize logs, alerts, and events generated by network devices, servers, applications, and security appliances into a unified dashboard or console, providing security teams with real-time visibility into potential security incidents, threats, and vulnerabilities. The deployment of a SIEM solution typically begins with planning and architecture design, identifying critical assets, network segments, and data sources that require monitoring using tools like `Splunk`, `QRadar`, or `ArcSight`, which offer scalable architectures and deployment options to accommodate organizational needs and IT environments.

Once the architecture is defined, organizations deploy SIEM agents or collectors on endpoints, servers, firewalls, and other network devices to collect and forward log data to the centralized SIEM platform for analysis and correlation using commands such as `Splunk Universal Forwarder` to deploy agents on endpoints or `QRadar DSM Editor` to configure device support modules for log collection and normalization from diverse network devices.

Moreover, SIEM systems leverage correlation rules, threat intelligence feeds, and machine learning algorithms to analyze incoming data streams and identify patterns indicative of security incidents or suspicious activities across the IT environment, enabling automated alert generation and prioritization based on predefined rules and behavioral baselines using `Splunk Search Processing Language (SPL)` or `QRadar Custom Rules` to create custom correlation rules and alerts based on specific threat indicators or attack patterns identified during threat intelligence feeds.

Additionally, SIEM platforms support real-time monitoring and incident response by providing dashboards, visualizations, and interactive analytics tools that enable security analysts to investigate security events, conduct forensic analysis, and respond to incidents promptly using `Splunk Dashboards` to visualize event data and `QRadar Offenses` to manage and prioritize security incidents based on severity and impact.

Furthermore, SIEM systems facilitate compliance management and auditing by generating reports, documenting security events, and providing audit trails for regulatory compliance requirements such as GDPR, PCI DSS, HIPAA, and SOX using `Splunk Enterprise Security` or `QRadar Compliance Modules` to automate compliance reporting and demonstrate adherence to industry standards and legal mandates.

Moreover, SIEM platforms integrate with Security Orchestration, Automation, and Response (SOAR) tools and Incident Response (IR) platforms to streamline incident response workflows, automate response actions, and orchestrate remediation efforts in response to security incidents or alerts using `Splunk Phantom` or `QRadar Incident Forensics` to automate incident response tasks, execute playbooks, and coordinate incident response efforts across the organization.

Additionally, SIEM solutions support threat hunting initiatives by enabling security teams to proactively search for indicators of compromise (IOCs), anomalous behaviors, or emerging threats within the IT environment using `Splunk Enterprise Security` or `QRadar Threat Hunting` to analyze historical data, conduct pattern searches, and identify potential security threats before they escalate into full-scale incidents.

Furthermore, SIEM systems enable log management and retention by providing scalable storage solutions, data archiving capabilities, and data lifecycle management policies to store and retrieve historical logs and security events for compliance, investigation, and forensic analysis using `Splunk SmartStore` or `QRadar Data Retention` to configure data retention policies, archival settings, and storage optimization strategies based on organizational requirements and regulatory mandates.

Moreover, SIEM platforms support cloud environments and hybrid deployments by integrating with cloud-native services, APIs, and logging mechanisms to collect and analyze security data from cloud platforms such as AWS, Azure, and Google Cloud using `Splunk Cloud` or `QRadar Cloud Pak for Security` to extend SIEM capabilities to cloud workloads, containers, and serverless applications with native integrations and cloud security posture management (CSPM) tools.

Additionally, SIEM solutions enhance threat intelligence capabilities by integrating with external threat intelligence feeds, threat feeds, and open-source intelligence (OSINT) sources to enrich security data, identify emerging threats, and enhance threat detection capabilities using `Splunk

Enterprise Security` or `QRadar Threat Intelligence App` to import threat feeds, integrate with threat intelligence platforms (TIPs), and correlate threat indicators with security events for proactive threat mitigation and defense.

Furthermore, SIEM platforms support anomaly detection and behavioral analysis by leveraging machine learning algorithms, statistical models, and user behavior analytics (UBA) to detect deviations from normal patterns of activity and identify insider threats, compromised accounts, or unusual network behavior using `Splunk User Behavior Analytics (UBA)` or `QRadar User Behavior Analytics` to analyze user activities, detect anomalous behaviors, and prioritize security incidents based on behavioral anomalies and risk scores.

Moreover, SIEM systems facilitate incident investigation and forensic analysis by providing search capabilities, data visualization tools, and forensic workflows to trace the origin of security incidents, reconstruct attack timelines, and gather evidence for incident response using `Splunk Investigate` or `QRadar Network Insights` to conduct forensic analysis, trace network traffic, and reconstruct attack scenarios based on correlated security events and log data.

In summary, implementing a SIEM solution is essential for organizations to enhance their cybersecurity defenses, achieve regulatory compliance, and improve incident response capabilities by centralizing security monitoring, automating threat detection and response, integrating with complementary security technologies, and providing real-time visibility into potential threats and vulnerabilities across the IT infrastructure. The integration of SIEM platforms with advanced analytics, threat intelligence feeds, and orchestration tools enables organizations to detect, respond to, and mitigate cyber threats effectively in today's complex and evolving threat landscape. Proactive threat detection strategies are critical components of modern cybersecurity frameworks, aimed at identifying and mitigating potential security threats before they escalate into full-scale incidents or breaches. These strategies leverage advanced technologies, threat intelligence, and proactive monitoring techniques to detect anomalous behaviors, suspicious activities, and emerging threats across networks, endpoints, applications, and data repositories. One of the key techniques in proactive threat detection is the deployment of Intrusion Detection Systems (IDS) and Intrusion Prevention Systems (IPS), which monitor network traffic and systems for signs of unauthorized access, malware infections, or suspicious activities using commands like `Snort` to deploy IDS rulesets or `Suricata` for network-based intrusion detection and prevention, enabling real-time alerting and blocking of malicious traffic.

Additionally, proactive threat detection strategies incorporate continuous vulnerability scanning and assessment to identify security weaknesses, misconfigurations, and potential entry points for attackers within the IT infrastructure using tools such as `Nessus`, `OpenVAS`, or `Qualys` to scan for vulnerabilities across network devices, servers, and applications, providing detailed reports and remediation recommendations based on scan results to prioritize patching and mitigation efforts using commands like `nmap -sV -O target_ip` to perform a vulnerability scan with version detection on the target IP address or `openvasmd --create-task="Scan Task" --target="Target IP"` to initiate a vulnerability scan task in

OpenVAS. Furthermore, proactive threat detection strategies involve leveraging threat intelligence feeds and threat hunting activities to identify and investigate potential threats based on indicators of compromise (IOCs), threat actor tactics, techniques, and procedures (TTPs), and emerging cybersecurity trends using platforms such as `MISP`, `ThreatConnect`, or `AlienVault OTX` to ingest and correlate threat intelligence data with security events and logs for proactive threat detection and response using `misp-galaxy` for threat hunting or `otx-pulse` to access threat intelligence feeds. Moreover, proactive threat detection strategies encompass anomaly detection and behavioral analytics techniques to detect deviations from normal patterns of user behavior, network traffic, and system activities indicative of insider threats, compromised accounts, or advanced persistent threats (APTs) using tools like `Splunk User Behavior Analytics (UBA)`, `Darktrace`, or `Cisco Stealthwatch` to analyze behavior anomalies and generate alerts based on behavioral baselines and machine learning algorithms using `splunk search "index=main | anomalydetection"` to search for anomalies in Splunk or `stealthwatch` to monitor network traffic and detect abnormal behaviors.

Additionally, proactive threat detection strategies involve implementing Security Information and Event Management (SIEM) systems to centralize log management, correlation, and real-time monitoring of security events across the IT infrastructure using platforms such as `Splunk Enterprise Security`, `IBM QRadar`, or `ArcSight` to collect, normalize, and analyze log data from diverse sources for threat detection, incident response, and compliance reporting using `splunk search index=main earliest=-1d@d latest=@d | stats count by sourcetype` to search and count log entries by sourcetype in Splunk or `ariel query "SELECT * FROM events WHERE event.category='Authentication' AND outcome='Failure'"` to query authentication failures in QRadar.

Furthermore, proactive threat detection strategies integrate Endpoint Detection and Response (EDR) solutions to monitor and respond to suspicious activities and malware infections on endpoints, servers, and mobile devices using platforms such as `CrowdStrike Falcon`, `Carbon Black`, or `Microsoft Defender for Endpoint` to collect telemetry data, perform behavioral analysis, and automate response actions using `falcon-sensor status` to check the status of CrowdStrike Falcon sensor or `cb defense status` to verify the status of Carbon Black agent on endpoints.

Moreover, proactive threat detection strategies include leveraging threat simulation and penetration testing exercises to assess and validate the effectiveness of cybersecurity defenses, incident response procedures, and mitigation strategies against simulated cyber attacks and scenarios using tools like `Metasploit`, `Cobalt Strike`, or `Nmap` to simulate attacker behavior, test network security controls, and identify vulnerabilities before adversaries can exploit them using `msfconsole` to launch Metasploit console or `nmap -sS -p 1-65535 target_ip` to perform a TCP SYN scan on target IP addresses for penetration testing.

Additionally, proactive threat detection strategies involve implementing deception technologies and honeypots to lure and detect attackers by deploying decoy systems, files, or network resources that mimic legitimate assets and services, allowing security teams to monitor and analyze attacker behavior and tactics without risking actual production environments using tools such as `KFSensor`, `Cymmetria MazeRunner`, or `DeceptionGrid` to deploy and manage deception environments for threat detection and incident response using `kfsensor.exe --start` to start KFSensor honeypot or `mazerunner` to deploy Cymmetria MazeRunner deception technology.

Furthermore, proactive threat detection strategies encompass leveraging Security Operations Centers (SOCs) and incident response teams to monitor, analyze, and respond to security incidents in real-time, leveraging automation, orchestration, and collaboration tools to streamline incident detection and response workflows across the organization using `TheHive`, `Demisto`, or `Splunk Phantom` to automate incident response tasks, orchestrate security workflows, and coordinate cross-functional teams using `thehive` command to start TheHive incident response platform or `phantom` to launch Splunk Phantom orchestration platform for automated incident handling.

In summary, proactive threat detection strategies are essential for organizations to anticipate, identify, and mitigate cybersecurity threats effectively, leveraging advanced technologies, threat intelligence, continuous monitoring, and response capabilities to protect sensitive data, ensure business continuity, and maintain trust with customers and stakeholders in today's evolving threat landscape. By integrating proactive threat detection techniques into comprehensive cybersecurity strategies, organizations can enhance their resilience against cyber threats and mitigate potential risks proactively.

Chapter 7: Advanced Malware Reverse Engineering

Dynamic analysis of malware samples is a crucial process in cybersecurity, involving the execution and observation of malicious software within a controlled environment to understand its behavior, functionality, and impact on systems and networks. This technique plays a vital role in threat intelligence, incident response, and malware research, providing insights into malware capabilities, infection vectors, and potential mitigation strategies. The process begins with setting up a secure and isolated environment such as a virtual machine (VM) or sandbox using tools like `VirtualBox`, `VMware`, or `QEMU` to create a controlled environment for malware analysis and execution, ensuring isolation from production systems and networks to prevent potential harm using `vboxmanage startvm "VM_name"` to start a VirtualBox VM or `qemu-system-x86_64 -hda malware_image.qcow2` to run a malware sample in a QEMU VM.

Furthermore, dynamic malware analysis involves capturing and monitoring the behavior of malware samples in real-time using tools like `Procmon` (Process Monitor), `Wireshark`, or `TCPDump` to monitor system calls, file system modifications, network traffic, and registry changes caused by the malware using `procmon.exe /accepteula /minimized` to start Process Monitor or `wireshark -i eth0` to capture network traffic on interface eth0 during malware execution.

Moreover, dynamic analysis techniques include analyzing the runtime behavior of malware samples to identify malicious activities such as system process manipulation, privilege

273

escalation attempts, or data exfiltration using `Process Explorer` or `Process Hacker` to examine process memory, threads, and handles associated with the malware using `procexp.exe` to analyze running processes or `procdump - ma PID dump_file.dmp` to create a memory dump of a specific process for further analysis.

Additionally, dynamic malware analysis involves capturing and analyzing network traffic generated by malware samples to identify command-and-control (C2) communications, data exfiltration, or malicious network behavior using tools like `Wireshark`, `tcpdump`, or `NetWitness` to capture and analyze network packets during malware execution using `wireshark -r malware.pcap` to analyze a pre-captured pcap file or `tcpdump -i eth0 -w capture.pcap` to capture live network traffic on interface eth0 for analysis.

Furthermore, dynamic analysis techniques encompass the use of debugging and disassembly tools such as `OllyDbg`, `IDA Pro`, or `Ghidra` to reverse engineer and analyze malware code, identify malicious functionalities, and uncover vulnerabilities or backdoor mechanisms embedded within the malware using `ida64.exe malware_sample.exe` to open a malware executable in IDA Pro or `ghidraRun` to launch Ghidra for analyzing malware binaries and scripts.

Moreover, dynamic malware analysis involves leveraging sandbox environments and automated malware analysis platforms such as `Cuckoo Sandbox`, `Joe Sandbox`, or `Hybrid Analysis` to automate the execution, analysis, and behavioral monitoring of malware samples using `cuckoo submit malware_sample.exe` to submit a malware sample for analysis or `joesandboxcli submit --file malware_sample.exe` to upload a malware sample to Joe Sandbox for automated analysis.

Additionally, dynamic analysis techniques include memory forensics and artifact analysis to extract and analyze volatile data such as process memory, registry keys, and network connections associated with malware execution using tools like `Volatility`, `Mandiant Redline`, or `Rekall` to analyze memory dumps and extract artifacts for further investigation using `volatility -f memory_dump.raw imageinfo` to identify the profile of a memory dump or `redline.exe collect -s` to collect system data for analysis with Mandiant Redline.

Furthermore, dynamic malware analysis involves behavioral profiling and pattern recognition techniques to classify malware samples based on their behavior, characteristics, and attack vectors using machine learning algorithms, clustering techniques, or signature-based detection methods to identify similarities and differences between malware families and variants using `YARA` rules or `ClamAV` signatures for pattern recognition and classification of malware samples based on behavior and characteristics.

Moreover, dynamic analysis techniques encompass dynamic code analysis and runtime instrumentation to monitor and intercept API calls, function hooks, or system events triggered by malware samples using tools like `API Monitor`, `Sysinternals Suite`, or `Detours` to intercept and analyze function calls, parameter values, and return results during malware execution using `apimonitor-x86.exe malware_sample.exe` to monitor API calls or `procmon64.exe -e malware_sample.exe` to monitor process activity and system events with Sysinternals Suite.

Additionally, dynamic malware analysis involves generating detailed reports and documentation of findings, including observed behaviors, artifacts, network indicators, and IOCs associated with malware samples using tools like `Maltego`, `MISP`, or `TheHive` to document and share analysis results, collaborate with incident response teams, and enhance threat intelligence using `maltegoce` to visualize relationships between IOCs or `thehive` to manage and analyze security incidents with TheHive incident response platform.

In summary, dynamic analysis of malware samples is a fundamental process in cybersecurity for understanding, detecting, and mitigating evolving threats, leveraging advanced tools, techniques, and methodologies to analyze malicious behaviors, identify attack vectors, and enhance defensive strategies. By integrating dynamic analysis techniques into comprehensive cybersecurity frameworks, organizations can strengthen their resilience against malware infections, improve incident response capabilities, and safeguard critical assets and sensitive information from sophisticated cyber threats in today's dynamic and evolving threat landscape. Code de-obfuscation techniques are essential in cybersecurity for unraveling obscured or obfuscated code designed to evade detection, analysis, or understanding by security researchers or defenders. Obfuscation is commonly used by malware authors and attackers to hide malicious intent, protect intellectual property, or deter reverse engineering efforts, necessitating effective methods to de-obfuscate and reveal the original logic and functionality of obfuscated code. One of the fundamental techniques in de-obfuscation involves manual code inspection and analysis using text editors like `vim`, `nano`, or `Sublime Text` to examine obfuscated code for patterns, anomalies, or suspicious constructs that may indicate obfuscation techniques such as string encryption, code packing, or control flow obfuscation using `vim obfuscated_code.c` to open an obfuscated C code file in Vim or `subl obfuscated_script.py` to analyze an obfuscated Python script in Sublime Text for identifying obfuscation patterns.

Additionally, automated de-obfuscation techniques leverage static analysis tools and de-obfuscation scripts to automate the process of unraveling obfuscated code, identifying and neutralizing obfuscation techniques using tools like `de4dot`, `Unicorn`, or `JEB Decompiler` to decompile, deobfuscate, and analyze obfuscated binaries, .NET assemblies, or Java applications using `de4dot input.exe -o output.exe` to deobfuscate a .NET executable or `jeb -c script.jeb` to load and deobfuscate a script file in JEB Decompiler for analyzing and understanding the original code structure and logic.

Moreover, dynamic analysis techniques involve executing obfuscated code within a controlled environment or sandbox using tools like `Cuckoo Sandbox`, `Joe Sandbox`, or `FireEye` to monitor runtime behavior, API calls, and system interactions to reveal hidden functionalities and malicious activities obscured by obfuscation using `cuckoo submit obfuscated_sample.exe` to submit an obfuscated executable for dynamic analysis in Cuckoo Sandbox or `joesandboxcli submit --file obfuscated_sample.exe` to upload an obfuscated sample to Joe Sandbox for automated behavioral analysis and de-obfuscation.

Furthermore, code de-obfuscation techniques include using pattern recognition and code similarity analysis to identify and categorize obfuscation patterns, frameworks, and libraries commonly employed by malware authors and attackers to obfuscate code using tools such as `YARA`, `Malware Analysis Sandbox`, or `Joxean Koret's PeStudio` to analyze and categorize obfuscation techniques based on code signatures, behaviors, and structural similarities using `yara -r rules.yar path_to_sample_directory` to scan and detect obfuscation patterns with YARA rules or `pestudio --source path_to_sample` to analyze obfuscation techniques in a binary file with Joxean Koret's PeStudio.

Additionally, code de-obfuscation techniques involve using script-based automation and custom scripts to decrypt, decode, or decompile obfuscated code, revealing hidden content, function calls, or logic obscured by obfuscation techniques such as base64 encoding, XOR encryption, or bytecode obfuscation using scripting languages like `Python`, `Ruby`, or `PowerShell` to automate de-obfuscation processes using `python deobfuscate_script.py` to execute a Python script for de-obfuscating malware code or `powershell -File deobfuscate.ps1` to run a PowerShell script for decrypting obfuscated PowerShell commands and scripts.

Moreover, code de-obfuscation techniques encompass leveraging machine learning and artificial intelligence (AI) algorithms to identify, classify, and deconstruct obfuscated code patterns and structures using techniques such as natural language processing (NLP), supervised learning, or deep learning models to recognize and interpret obfuscation techniques in code using machine learning frameworks like `TensorFlow`, `scikit-learn`, or `PyTorch` to train models for detecting and de-obfuscating malware using `tensorflow` to build and train deep learning models or `scikit-learn` for supervised learning algorithms to classify obfuscated code patterns and structures.

Additionally, code de-obfuscation techniques involve leveraging online and community-driven resources such as malware analysis forums, code repositories, and threat intelligence platforms to share knowledge, tools, and techniques for de-obfuscating malware and understanding obfuscation strategies used by threat actors using platforms like `GitHub`, `VirusTotal`, or `Malwarebytes Forums` to access and contribute to open-source de-obfuscation tools, scripts, and analysis techniques using `github.com` to search for de-obfuscation scripts or tools in public repositories or `virustotal.com` to analyze and detect obfuscated code patterns in malware samples.

Furthermore, code de-obfuscation techniques encompass collaborative efforts and information sharing among cybersecurity professionals, researchers, and organizations to collectively analyze and mitigate obfuscated threats, leveraging collaborative platforms like `TheHive`, `MISP`, or `ThreatConnect` to share threat intelligence, analysis results, and de-obfuscation techniques for proactive threat detection and response using `thehive` to manage and analyze security incidents with TheHive incident response platform or `misp-galaxy` to exchange and correlate obfuscation indicators with MISP threat intelligence platform for enhancing malware analysis and de-obfuscation capabilities.

In summary, code de-obfuscation techniques are essential for cybersecurity professionals and researchers to unravel obscured or obfuscated code used by malware authors and attackers to evade detection and analysis, leveraging a combination of manual inspection, automated tools, dynamic analysis, pattern recognition, machine learning, and collaborative efforts to uncover hidden functionalities, malicious behaviors, and vulnerabilities obscured by obfuscation techniques. By employing effective de-obfuscation strategies and leveraging advanced technologies, organizations can enhance their ability to detect, analyze, and mitigate obfuscated threats, protect sensitive data, and safeguard against evolving cyber threats in today's complex and dynamic threat landscape.

Chapter 8: Forensic Analysis of Encrypted Data

Techniques for decrypting encrypted data are essential in cybersecurity and digital forensics for recovering plaintext information from ciphertext using various methods and tools to bypass encryption algorithms, recover keys, or exploit vulnerabilities in encryption implementations. One of the fundamental techniques in decrypting encrypted data involves brute-force attacks, where exhaustive search methods are used to try all possible keys until the correct one is found, applicable especially in scenarios where weak encryption algorithms or short key lengths are used, using tools like `John the Ripper`, `hashcat`, or `Aircrack-ng` to perform brute-force attacks on encrypted data using `john --format=DES ciphertext.txt` to crack DES encrypted data or `hashcat -m 1800 -a 3 hashfile.txt rockyou.txt` for attacking a hash using a wordlist.

Additionally, dictionary attacks are another technique used for decrypting encrypted data by systematically trying words or phrases from a predefined list (dictionary) of commonly used passwords or phrases, leveraging tools such as `Hydra`, `Medusa`, or `Cain and Abel` to perform dictionary attacks against encrypted files, passwords, or digital certificates using `hydra -l username -P password_list.txt ftp://target_ip` to launch a dictionary attack against an FTP server or `medusa -h target_ip -U users.txt -P passwords.txt -M ftp` to perform a similar attack with Medusa.

Moreover, rainbow table attacks are employed for decrypting encrypted data by precomputing hash values of plaintext passwords and storing them in a table (rainbow table), enabling rapid lookup and recovery of plaintext passwords from hashed values, using tools like `RainbowCrack`, `Ophcrack`, or `Rainbow Tables` to crack hashed passwords or encrypted data using `rtgen hash_algorithm charset_length -f rainbowtable_path` to generate a rainbow table or `rainbowcrack plaintext hash_table.txt` to decrypt an encrypted hash using a rainbow table.

Furthermore, decryption techniques involve leveraging known plaintext or chosen plaintext attacks to decrypt encrypted data by exploiting cryptographic weaknesses, such as improper use of encryption algorithms, predictable patterns in plaintext, or side-channel attacks, using specialized tools and scripts tailored for specific cryptographic vulnerabilities and attack vectors, such as `Cryptool`, `OpenSSL`, or custom Python scripts to exploit weaknesses in encryption algorithms using `openssl enc -d -aes-256-cbc -in encrypted_file.txt -out decrypted_file.txt -k passphrase` for decrypting AES encrypted data or `python custom_decryptor.py encrypted_data.txt` to execute a custom Python script for decrypting specific encrypted data.

Additionally, cryptographic flaws in encryption algorithms or implementation errors can be exploited using cryptanalysis techniques to recover plaintext from ciphertext without knowledge of the encryption key, relying on mathematical analysis, statistical methods, or known vulnerabilities in cryptographic protocols, using tools such as `Wireshark`, `John the Ripper`, or `CrypTool` for analyzing encrypted traffic, brute-forcing passwords, or exploiting cryptographic weaknesses using `wireshark -o decryption.ikev2_decryption_keys:"IKEv2 Pre-Shared Keys" -r encrypted_traffic.pcap` to analyze IKEv2 encrypted traffic or `crypTool` for analyzing cryptographic protocols and vulnerabilities.

Moreover, decryption techniques involve reverse engineering and analyzing encryption algorithms or custom cryptographic implementations to uncover weaknesses, backdoors, or flaws that can be exploited to decrypt encrypted data using `IDA Pro`, `Ghidra`, or `OllyDbg` for disassembling, debugging, and analyzing executable files, firmware, or custom applications using `ida64.exe encrypted_binary.exe` to analyze an encrypted binary file in IDA Pro or `ollydbg encrypted_process.exe` to debug an encrypted process in OllyDbg for identifying encryption routines and understanding encryption mechanisms.

Furthermore, decryption techniques encompass leveraging quantum computing algorithms and quantum computers to perform Shor's algorithm or Grover's algorithm for decrypting encrypted data using quantum computing principles to factorize large prime numbers or search for cryptographic keys faster than classical computers, enabling decryption of encrypted data encrypted with RSA or symmetric key algorithms using `IBM Qiskit`, `D-Wave Systems`, or `Microsoft Q#` to develop and execute quantum algorithms for decrypting encrypted data or breaking cryptographic keys using `qiskit` to simulate and execute quantum algorithms in IBM Qiskit framework.

Additionally, decryption techniques involve leveraging side-channel attacks, timing attacks, or fault injection techniques to exploit physical or implementation vulnerabilities in encryption devices or systems to recover plaintext from ciphertext without knowledge of the encryption key, using specialized hardware tools, oscilloscopes, or electromagnetic analysis equipment for analyzing cryptographic devices or smart cards using `ChipWhisperer`, `JTAGulator`, or `Logic Analyzer` to perform side-channel attacks or fault injections on cryptographic devices for recovering encryption keys or decrypting encrypted data.

Moreover, decryption techniques encompass leveraging collaborative efforts, research, and information sharing among cybersecurity professionals, researchers, and organizations to collectively develop, refine, and apply decryption techniques and tools for analyzing and mitigating encrypted threats, using platforms such as `GitHub`, `Cryptohack`, or `CyberChef` for sharing decryption scripts, techniques, and tools using `github.com` to access and contribute to open-source decryption tools or `cyberchef` to develop and share custom decryption pipelines and recipes for analyzing and decrypting encrypted data.

In summary, techniques for decrypting encrypted data are essential for cybersecurity professionals and researchers to analyze, identify vulnerabilities, and mitigate threats posed by encrypted communications, files, or data, leveraging a combination of brute-force attacks, dictionary attacks, cryptanalysis, reverse engineering, quantum computing, and specialized techniques to recover plaintext from ciphertext, uncover cryptographic weaknesses, and enhance defensive strategies against evolving encryption-based threats in today's digital landscapeCryptographic key recovery methods are crucial in cybersecurity and cryptography for retrieving lost, forgotten, or compromised keys used in encryption and decryption processes, essential for accessing encrypted data or securing communications without the original key, employing various techniques and tools tailored to different cryptographic algorithms, protocols, and scenarios. One of the primary methods in cryptographic key recovery involves brute-force attacks, where exhaustive search methods are employed to try all possible combinations until the correct key is found, suitable for scenarios where weak key lengths or passwords are used, using tools like `John the Ripper`, `hashcat`, or `Aircrack-ng` for cracking passwords or keys with brute force, such as `john --format=DES encrypted_data.txt` for DES encryption or `hashcat -m 1000 hashfile.txt rockyou.txt` for attacking MD5 hashes with a wordlist.

Furthermore, dictionary attacks are utilized to recover cryptographic keys by systematically testing words or phrases from a predefined list (dictionary) of commonly used passwords or key phrases, employing tools such as `Hydra`, `Medusa`, or `Cain and Abel` to perform dictionary attacks against encrypted files, digital certificates, or password hashes, using `hydra -l username -P password_list.txt ftp://target_ip` to launch a dictionary attack against an FTP server or `medusa -h target_ip -U users.txt -P passwords.txt -M ftp` to perform a similar attack with Medusa.

Additionally, rainbow table attacks are employed for cryptographic key recovery by precomputing hash values of plaintext passwords and storing them in a table (rainbow table) for rapid lookup and recovery of plaintext passwords or cryptographic keys from hashed values, leveraging tools like `RainbowCrack`, `Ophcrack`, or `Rainbow Tables` to crack hashed passwords or encrypted data using `rtgen hash_algorithm charset_length -f rainbowtable_path` to generate a rainbow table or `rainbowcrack plaintext hash_table.txt` to decrypt an encrypted hash using a rainbow table.

Moreover, cryptographic key recovery techniques involve leveraging known plaintext or chosen plaintext attacks to recover cryptographic keys by exploiting weaknesses in encryption algorithms, protocols, or implementation errors, employing specialized tools and scripts tailored for specific cryptographic vulnerabilities and attack vectors, such as `Cryptool`, `OpenSSL`, or custom Python scripts to exploit weaknesses in encryption algorithms using `openssl enc -d -aes-256-cbc -in encrypted_file.txt -out decrypted_file.txt -k passphrase` for decrypting AES encrypted data or `python custom_decryptor.py encrypted_data.txt` to execute a custom Python script for recovering specific encrypted data.

Furthermore, cryptanalysis techniques are used for cryptographic key recovery by analyzing the structure, patterns, and properties of cryptographic algorithms to discover vulnerabilities, backdoors, or flaws that can be exploited to recover cryptographic keys, employing tools such as `Wireshark`, `John the Ripper`, or `CrypTool` for analyzing encrypted traffic, brute-forcing passwords, or exploiting cryptographic weaknesses using `wireshark -o decryption.ikev2_decryption_keys:"IKEv2 Pre-Shared Keys" -r encrypted_traffic.pcap` to analyze IKEv2 encrypted traffic or `crypTool` for analyzing cryptographic protocols and vulnerabilities.

Moreover, cryptographic key recovery involves reverse engineering and analyzing cryptographic algorithms, custom cryptographic implementations, or hardware security modules (HSMs) to uncover vulnerabilities, backdoors, or flaws that can be exploited to recover cryptographic keys using tools like `IDA Pro`, `Ghidra`, or `OllyDbg` for disassembling, debugging, and analyzing executable files, firmware, or custom applications using `ida64.exe encrypted_binary.exe` to analyze an encrypted binary file in IDA Pro or `ollydbg encrypted_process.exe` to debug an encrypted process in OllyDbg for identifying encryption routines and understanding encryption mechanisms.

Additionally, quantum computing algorithms such as Shor's algorithm or Grover's algorithm are employed for cryptographic key recovery, exploiting quantum computing principles to factorize large prime numbers or search for cryptographic keys faster than classical computers, enabling decryption of encrypted data encrypted with RSA or symmetric key algorithms using `IBM Qiskit`, `D-Wave Systems`, or `Microsoft Q#` to develop and execute quantum algorithms for decrypting encrypted data or breaking cryptographic keys using `qiskit` to simulate and execute quantum algorithms in IBM Qiskit framework.

Furthermore, cryptographic key recovery techniques encompass leveraging side-channel attacks, timing attacks, or fault injection techniques to exploit physical or implementation vulnerabilities in cryptographic devices or systems to recover cryptographic keys or decrypt encrypted data using specialized hardware tools, oscilloscopes, or electromagnetic analysis equipment for analyzing cryptographic devices or smart cards using `ChipWhisperer`, `JTAGulator`, or `Logic Analyzer` to perform side-channel attacks or fault injections on cryptographic devices for recovering encryption keys or decrypting encrypted data.

Moreover, collaborative efforts, research, and information sharing among cybersecurity professionals, researchers, and organizations are essential for developing, refining, and applying cryptographic key recovery techniques and tools for analyzing and mitigating encrypted threats, using platforms such as `GitHub`, `Cryptohack`, or `CyberChef` for sharing cryptographic key recovery scripts, techniques, and tools using `github.com` to access and contribute to open-source cryptographic key recovery tools or `cyberchef` to develop and share custom cryptographic key recovery pipelines and recipes for analyzing and recovering cryptographic keys.

In summary, cryptographic key recovery methods are essential for cybersecurity professionals and researchers to recover lost, forgotten, or compromised cryptographic keys used in encryption and decryption processes, employing a combination of brute-force attacks, dictionary attacks, rainbow table attacks, cryptanalysis, reverse engineering, quantum computing, side-channel attacks, and collaborative efforts to enhance cryptographic key recovery capabilities and mitigate risks associated with encrypted communications, files, or data in today's digital landscape.

Chapter 9: Incident Response in Industrial Control Systems (ICS)

Security challenges and risks in Industrial Control Systems (ICS) environments are critical concerns that pose significant threats to operational technology (OT) infrastructure, industrial processes, and critical infrastructure sectors worldwide, necessitating comprehensive understanding, mitigation strategies, and ongoing vigilance to protect against cyber threats and vulnerabilities. One of the primary security challenges in ICS environments is the convergence of IT (Information Technology) and OT (Operational Technology) networks, where traditional IT security measures and protocols may not adequately address the unique requirements and vulnerabilities inherent in OT systems, leading to potential exposure to cyber attacks and disruptions in industrial operations.

Moreover, legacy systems and equipment used in ICS environments often lack built-in security features, such as encryption, authentication mechanisms, or regular security updates, making them vulnerable to exploitation by threat actors who exploit known vulnerabilities or weaknesses in outdated software and firmware versions, requiring organizations to prioritize patch management and risk mitigation strategies using tools like `Nessus`, `OpenVAS`, or `Qualys` for vulnerability scanning and assessment in ICS environments to identify and remediate security vulnerabilities.

Additionally, the complexity and interdependencies of interconnected ICS components and systems, including Supervisory Control and Data Acquisition (SCADA) systems,

Programmable Logic Controllers (PLCs), and Human-Machine Interfaces (HMIs), create attack surfaces that can be exploited by adversaries to manipulate or disrupt industrial processes, necessitating comprehensive network segmentation, access control, and intrusion detection mechanisms using `iptables`, `pfSense`, or `FirewallD` for configuring network segmentation and firewall rules in ICS environments to restrict unauthorized access and prevent lateral movement of attackers.

Furthermore, the critical nature of ICS environments, where disruptions or compromises can lead to physical damage, safety hazards, environmental impacts, or financial losses, underscores the importance of resilience and incident response preparedness in mitigating security risks and minimizing operational downtime using incident response frameworks like `NIST SP 800-82`, `ICS-CERT`, or `SANS ICS` for developing and implementing incident response plans specific to ICS environments to ensure timely detection, containment, and recovery from cybersecurity incidents.

Moreover, the lack of cybersecurity awareness and skilled personnel in ICS environments poses a significant challenge, as many operators, engineers, and technicians may not have adequate training or expertise in identifying and responding to cyber threats effectively, highlighting the need for continuous training, education, and capacity building initiatives using training resources like `ICS-CERT`, `SANS ICS`, or `ISA/IEC 62443` for cybersecurity training and certification programs tailored to ICS security requirements and best practices.

Additionally, the proliferation of interconnected devices and Industrial Internet of Things (IIoT) devices in ICS environments introduces new vectors for cyber attacks, as these devices often have limited security features, firmware vulnerabilities, or default credentials that can be exploited by adversaries to gain unauthorized access or launch attacks, requiring organizations to implement robust IoT device management and security protocols using `IoT Inspector`, `Shodan`, or `Metasploit` for scanning and identifying vulnerable IoT devices in ICS networks to mitigate security risks and strengthen overall cybersecurity posture.

Furthermore, supply chain risks in ICS environments pose significant threats, as third-party vendors, contractors, or suppliers may introduce vulnerabilities or malicious components into the supply chain, compromising the integrity and security of ICS systems and operations, necessitating rigorous supplier vetting, procurement policies, and supply chain security assessments using tools like `Burp Suite`, `OWASP ZAP`, or `Supply Chain Risk Management` frameworks to assess and mitigate supply chain risks in ICS environments.

Moreover, the increasing sophistication and persistence of cyber threats targeting ICS environments, such as ransomware, advanced persistent threats (APTs), or insider threats, underscore the need for continuous monitoring, threat intelligence sharing, and proactive defense strategies using threat intelligence platforms like `MISP`, `ThreatConnect`, or `Cyber Threat Intelligence` services for aggregating, analyzing, and disseminating threat intelligence specific to ICS threats and vulnerabilities to preemptively detect and respond to emerging cyber threats.

Additionally, regulatory compliance requirements and industry standards, such as NERC CIP, ISA/IEC 62443, or

GDPR, impose additional challenges on ICS operators and organizations to ensure compliance with cybersecurity regulations, data protection requirements, and privacy mandates while maintaining operational resilience and security using compliance frameworks and assessment tools like `NERC CIP Auditor`, `ISA/IEC 62443 Toolkit`, or `GDPR Compliance Checklist` for auditing and validating compliance with regulatory requirements in ICS environments.

Furthermore, geopolitical tensions and cyber warfare tactics pose evolving threats to ICS environments, as nation-state actors and cybercriminal groups increasingly target critical infrastructure sectors for espionage, sabotage, or disruption purposes, necessitating robust cybersecurity strategies, threat modeling, and international cooperation initiatives using diplomatic channels, cybersecurity alliances, or collaborative frameworks like `CIS Controls`, `EU Cyber Diplomacy Toolbox`, or `International Cybersecurity Cooperation` agreements for addressing cross-border cyber threats and ensuring global cybersecurity resilience.

In summary, addressing security challenges and risks in ICS environments requires a holistic approach encompassing technical measures, governance frameworks, workforce development, threat intelligence sharing, regulatory compliance, and international cooperation to enhance cybersecurity resilience, protect critical infrastructure, and safeguard industrial operations against evolving cyber threats in an interconnected and digitalized world

Chapter 10: Case Studies and Lessons Learned

Real-world incident response case studies provide invaluable insights into how organizations detect, respond to, and recover from cybersecurity incidents, offering practical lessons, best practices, and methodologies for handling various cyber threats and attacks effectively, illustrating the application of incident response frameworks, techniques, and tools in diverse organizational contexts and industries. One notable case study involves the 2017 Equifax data breach, where unauthorized access to sensitive personal information of over 147 million individuals was compromised due to a vulnerability in Apache Struts, highlighting the importance of vulnerability management and patching procedures using tools like `Nessus`, `OpenVAS`, or `Qualys` for vulnerability scanning and assessment to identify and mitigate vulnerabilities before they are exploited by attackers.

Another significant incident response case study is the WannaCry ransomware attack in 2017, which affected hundreds of thousands of computers worldwide by exploiting a vulnerability in the Windows SMB protocol, demonstrating the rapid spread and impact of ransomware threats in critical sectors such as healthcare and manufacturing, emphasizing the importance of timely patching and incident response readiness using tools like `Microsoft Security Update`, `EternalBlue Exploit`, or `Metasploit` for exploiting SMB vulnerability to deploy ransomware on vulnerable systems.

Moreover, the NotPetya cyber attack in 2017 targeted Ukrainian financial, energy, and government sectors, spreading globally and causing significant operational disruptions and financial losses to multinational companies, highlighting the destructive capabilities of state-sponsored malware and the importance of robust backup and recovery strategies using tools like `Acronis True Image`, `Veeam Backup & Replication`, or `Backup Exec` for creating and managing backups to restore critical data and systems in case of ransomware or malware attacks.

Additionally, the SolarWinds supply chain attack in 2020 compromised software updates distributed by SolarWinds Orion, allowing threat actors to infiltrate numerous government agencies and private organizations, underscoring the risks posed by supply chain vulnerabilities and the importance of supply chain risk management using tools like `Burp Suite`, `OWASP ZAP`, or `Supply Chain Risk Management` frameworks for assessing and mitigating supply chain risks through vulnerability scanning and security assessments.

Furthermore, the 2015 breach of Ashley Madison, a dating website for extramarital affairs, exposed sensitive user data and led to widespread reputational damage and legal repercussions for the company, highlighting the significance of data protection measures, privacy regulations compliance, and incident response planning using frameworks like `GDPR`, `HIPAA`, or `PCI DSS` for ensuring data privacy and regulatory compliance through comprehensive security policies and procedures.

Moreover, the Stuxnet cyber attack in 2010 targeted Iran's nuclear facilities, leveraging zero-day vulnerabilities in Siemens PLCs to sabotage centrifuges used for uranium enrichment, illustrating the convergence of cyber warfare tactics and industrial control systems (ICS) vulnerabilities, emphasizing the need for advanced threat detection and mitigation strategies using tools like `Wireshark`, `Snort`, or `Suricata` for network traffic analysis and intrusion detection in ICS environments to detect and respond to cyber threats.

Additionally, the 2014 Sony Pictures Entertainment hack resulted in the theft and disclosure of sensitive corporate data, internal communications, and unreleased films, attributed to North Korean state-sponsored actors in retaliation for the film "The Interview," demonstrating the geopolitical motivations behind cyber attacks and the importance of threat intelligence sharing and collaboration using platforms like `MISP`, `ThreatConnect`, or `Cyber Threat Intelligence` services for aggregating, analyzing, and disseminating threat intelligence to preemptively detect and respond to cyber threats.

Furthermore, the 2013 Target data breach compromised payment card information of millions of customers due to a malware infection on the retailer's point-of-sale systems, illustrating the risks posed by malware attacks and the critical role of endpoint detection and response (EDR) solutions using tools like `CrowdStrike Falcon`, `Carbon Black`, or `FireEye Endpoint Security` for real-time detection, investigation, and response to malicious activities on endpoints and networks.

Moreover, the 2016 Democratic National Committee (DNC) email leak involved the compromise of confidential emails and documents, attributed to Russian state-sponsored hackers, influencing the 2016 U.S. presidential election, underscoring the impact of cyber attacks on political institutions and democratic processes, emphasizing the importance of email security, phishing awareness training, and incident response readiness using `PhishMe`, `KnowBe4`, or `Proofpoint` for simulating phishing attacks and training employees to recognize and report suspicious emails.

In summary, real-world incident response case studies provide valuable lessons and insights into the evolving landscape of cybersecurity threats, highlighting the importance of proactive cybersecurity measures, incident response planning, threat detection technologies, and collaboration across industries and sectors to effectively detect, mitigate, and recover from cyber attacks, ensuring resilience, security, and continuity in the face of emerging and persistent cyber threats in today's interconnected digital ecosystem. Extracting lessons learned from incident response exercises is a critical aspect of refining and enhancing organizational readiness and resilience against cyber threats and security incidents, involving the systematic analysis, evaluation, and documentation of simulated scenarios to identify strengths, weaknesses, and areas for improvement in incident response plans, procedures, and capabilities, using frameworks like `NIST SP 800-61`, `SANS Incident Handling`, or `ISO/IEC 27035` for conducting incident response exercises and documenting lessons learned to enhance incident response effectiveness and readiness.

One of the primary techniques for extracting lessons learned from incident response exercises involves conducting thorough after-action reviews (AARs) using tools such as `AAR Toolkit`, `After Action Review`, or `JIRA` for capturing and documenting observations, insights, and recommendations from participants and stakeholders involved in simulated incidents to identify gaps, bottlenecks, and areas requiring improvement in incident response procedures and coordination using `JIRA` to create action items and assign tasks for remediation based on AAR findings or `After Action Review` for conducting structured reviews to analyze incident response performance.

Moreover, documenting incident response exercise outcomes and findings using `SharePoint`, `Confluence`, or `Wiki` for creating detailed reports, dashboards, or knowledge bases to centralize incident response lessons learned, best practices, and recommendations for organizational reference and continuous improvement in incident response capabilities and resilience using `Confluence` for collaborative documentation and `SharePoint` for centralized storage and sharing of incident response exercise reports and findings.

Furthermore, conducting scenario-based tabletop exercises or red team-blue team simulations using tools like `Cobalt Strike`, `CALDERA`, or `Metta` for simulating cyber attacks and testing incident response capabilities, enabling participants to practice detection, containment, and mitigation strategies against realistic threats and scenarios to validate incident response plans and procedures using `Cobalt Strike` for conducting red team operations or `Metta` for executing adversarial simulation scenarios.
Additionally, leveraging automation and orchestration tools for incident response exercises and simulations using `SOAR` (Security Orchestration, Automation, and Response) platforms like `Demisto`, `Splunk Phantom`, or `Siemplify` for automating incident response workflows, orchestrating security operations, and integrating with security tools and systems to streamline response efforts and improve incident

response efficiency and effectiveness using `Splunk Phantom` for automating playbook execution or `Demisto` for orchestrating incident response processes.

Moreover, integrating threat intelligence feeds and real-time data sources into incident response exercises using platforms like `MISP`, `ThreatConnect`, or `AlienVault OTX` for enriching simulated scenarios with relevant threat intelligence, indicators of compromise (IOCs), and adversary tactics, techniques, and procedures (TTPs) to enhance realism and complexity in incident response simulations and exercises using `ThreatConnect` for integrating threat intelligence feeds or `MISP` for sharing and correlating threat intelligence during incident response exercises.

Furthermore, fostering a culture of continuous learning and improvement in incident response capabilities through regular training, workshops, and knowledge sharing sessions using `Cybrary`, `InfoSec Institute`, or `SANS Institute` for cybersecurity training and certification programs tailored to incident response roles and responsibilities, ensuring that personnel are equipped with the latest skills, knowledge, and techniques to effectively respond to cyber incidents using `SANS Institute` for incident response training or `InfoSec Institute` for specialized cybersecurity courses.

Additionally, establishing cross-functional collaboration and communication channels between IT (Information Technology), OT (Operational Technology), legal, compliance, and executive stakeholders during incident response exercises using `Slack`, `Microsoft Teams`, or `Zoom` for real-time communication, coordination, and decision-making to enhance incident response coordination and alignment with organizational objectives and priorities using `Microsoft Teams` for incident response collaboration or `Zoom` for conducting virtual incident response tabletop exercises.

Moreover, conducting post-mortem analysis and continuous improvement reviews following incident response exercises using `Root Cause Analysis (RCA)`, `DevOps practices`, or `Continuous Improvement` frameworks for identifying systemic issues, root causes, and corrective actions to prevent recurrence of incidents and enhance overall incident response effectiveness and resilience using `DevOps practices` for implementing automation and continuous improvement in incident response processes or `Root Cause Analysis (RCA)` for analyzing incident root causes and implementing preventive measures.

In summary, extracting lessons learned from incident response exercises involves a systematic approach to analyzing and documenting insights, recommendations, and improvements to enhance organizational readiness and resilience against cyber threats and security incidents, leveraging tools, frameworks, and best practices for continuous learning, collaboration, and improvement in incident response capabilities and effectiveness in today's dynamic and evolving threat landscape

Conclusion

In summary, "Cyber Incident Response: Counterintelligence and Forensics for Security Investigators" offers a comprehensive journey through the fundamentals, techniques, strategies, and advanced methods essential for mastering cyber incident response. Across four meticulously crafted books, this bundle equips both beginners and seasoned professionals alike with the knowledge and skills necessary to navigate the complexities of cybersecurity threats and forensic investigations.

Book 1, "Cyber Incident Response Fundamentals: A Beginner's Guide to Counterintelligence and Forensics," lays a solid foundation by introducing key concepts, methodologies, and best practices in cyber incident response. It serves as an essential primer for understanding the evolving threat landscape and developing foundational skills in cybersecurity investigations.

Building upon this groundwork, Book 2, "Intermediate Cyber Forensics: Techniques and Tools for Security Investigators," delves deeper into advanced techniques and forensic tools used by security investigators. Readers learn to leverage cutting-edge technologies and methodologies to detect, analyze, and respond effectively to cyber incidents, ensuring a robust defense against malicious actors.

Book 3, "Advanced Counterintelligence Strategies: Expert Methods in Cyber Incident Response," elevates the discussion to expert-level strategies and tactics employed by elite security investigators. It explores sophisticated counterintelligence strategies, threat hunting techniques, and proactive defense measures designed to thwart complex cyber threats and mitigate risks effectively.

Finally, Book 4, "Mastering Cyber Incident Response: Comprehensive Techniques for Elite Security Investigators," synthesizes the knowledge and experiences gained throughout the series. It provides comprehensive insights into orchestrating seamless incident response operations, integrating threat intelligence, and applying forensic methodologies to achieve swift resolution and minimize organizational impact during cybersecurity crises.

Together, these books not only educate but empower security professionals to adapt to the ever-changing cybersecurity landscape with confidence and agility. By embracing a holistic approach to cyber incident response, readers are equipped to safeguard critical assets, uphold data integrity, and preserve organizational resilience in the face of relentless cyber threats.

"Cyber Incident Response: Counterintelligence and Forensics for Security Investigators" is not just a series of books; it is a vital resource and guide for anyone committed to mastering the art and science of cyber incident response in today's digital age. Whether you are embarking on your cybersecurity journey or seeking to enhance your expertise, this bundle provides the essential knowledge and tools to excel in defending against, responding to, and mitigating the impact of cyber incidents.

www.ingramcontent.com/pod-product-compliance
Lightning Source LLC
Chambersburg PA
CBHW071234050326
40690CB00011B/2112